MW01611287

QUICK PREP CAREERS

▶▶

GOOD JOBS IN ONE YEAR OR LESS

PAUL PHIFER

MJF BOOKS
NEW YORK

Published by MJF Books
Fine Communications
322 Eighth Avenue
New York, NY 10001

Quick Prep Careers: Good Jobs in One Year or Less
LC Control Number 2006937792
ISBN-13: 978-1-56731-859-3
ISBN-10: 1-56731-859-2

This edition is published by MJF Books in arrangement with
Infobase Publishing Inc. Originally published by Ferguson
Publishing Company, an Infobase Publishing company.

Editor: Carol Yehling
Proofreader: Jonathan Bieniek

Printed in the United States of America.

MJF Books and the MJF colophon are trademarks of Fine Creative
Media, Inc.

QM   10   9   8   7   6   5   4   3   2   1

TABLE OF CONTENTS

Acknowledgments

I would like to extend my sincere appreciation to the Ferguson Publishing staff for their continuing support and technical enrichment of the projects I have submitted; to the many clients, authors, writers, and others I was privileged to draw upon, all of whose names I was unable to include in the bibliographies; to Mitch Nagel, for allowing me to use his summary sheet as an example; and finally, and most importantly, for God's mercy, grace, and empowering ability that enabled me to complete this sharing effort.

Dedication

To my wife, Margaret, for her continuing support, love, and patience, particularly during those times when deadlines kept me preoccupied.

INTRODUCTION

Who comes to tow your car out of that ditch you have just
   skidded into?

Who drives children to and from school each day?

Who types the office correspondence and records and files
   copies so you can find them?

Who prepares and serves the food at your favorite
   restaurants?

Who finds the broken connection caused by an ice storm
   and restores your electrical power?

Who repairs the furnace? Hot water heater? Washer and
   dryer?

Who cares for children while their parents are at work?

Who cares for the elderly and others who live in assisted living centers and nursing homes?

Who removes the garbage from your curb?

Who helps you find a pair of jeans that fit and then rings up
   your purchase?

All of these "who's" are people who work in jobs that require a year
or less of training and preparation, jobs that often are not considered great jobs, or even good jobs. That's an unfortunate miscon-
ception because these jobs are of great value to millions of employees' lives and careers. They are of great importance to employers.
And our society would come to a standstill without them.

   During the 2000 presidential campaign, a common utterance
by one of the candidates was; "Ask yourself: Are you better off
today than you were eight years ago?" While not explicitly stated,
it appeared the objective was to have each voter look at his or her
financial status and materialistic accumulations and determine if
life is better now than it was before. However, a higher-paying
job, increased fringe benefits, and more material goods are not the
only indicators of a better life. You can have all that and still be
unfocused and unfulfilled.

   Too many Americans still believe that the road to financial
and social success begins with a bachelor's degree. Although it is
hard for parents, educators, and students to accept it, the fact is
that most jobs in America do not now, and will not in the foresee-

able future, require a bachelor's degree or more to perform. Too many people believe that a bachelor's degree is required for any hope of success and take on an overwhelming combination of activities in an effort to obtain this cherished prize. The combination of school, work, financial, and family commitments too often results in stress, discouragement, and academic failure for a large percentage of those who begin to pursue a bachelor's degree. Of course, some individuals can and should earn a college degree, but it's not a good choice for everyone. Furthermore, it is unlikely our society could provide occupations for everyone if all of those who started a bachelor's degree program successfully completed their requirements. America needs millions of people who are able and willing to work in the jobs that require a year or less of preparation.

Quick Prep Careers looks at 50 Good Jobs that require a year or less of preparation to enter. They are Good Jobs in terms of their value to a person's life and career direction, to employers, and to society.

This book also includes profiles of 25 jobs that can be enhanced through certification programs that take a year or less or complete. There is a growing trend toward job enhancement or complementing a degree through additional training at the post-associate's and bachelor's degree levels. This trend seems to be due partly to growing competition in selected job areas. In addition, employers increasingly need workers with advanced proficiency to produce higher-quality products and services, and they are often willing to pay for the additional training it takes to achieve their goals.

Who Will Find This Book Helpful?

STUDENTS
(Includes students of all ethnic, cultural, and economic backgrounds, including those with disabilities)

- Shows how jobs that traditionally have not been viewed as good make positive contributions to the employer, society, and the student's overall life direction

- Gives purpose and meaning to jobs that are not generally considered important

- Provides a big-picture or a life-direction view of part-time and/or temporary work, often viewed as having little importance in the long run

- Attempts to show the importance of attitude in terms of whether a job will be perceived as good
- Shows how certification can enhance or complement the work/life situation of students who have earned a postsecondary degree

PARENTS

(Includes foster parents, grandparents, or guardians who have significant responsibility for supporting or guiding one or more individuals)

- Helps parents encourage youths and young adults who are not college bound but need support in their pursuit of worthwhile and important work endeavors
- Provides clear reasons why a job can be considered good in spite of prevailing opinions and beliefs
- Helps parents develop and promote healthy and supportive attitudes toward work that they may have considered less than desirable by clearly stating the benefits for society and positive contributions to the overall growth of their children
- Introduces the short-term certificate option as a viable alternative to a traditional degree program
- Provides parents and guardians the information they need to support their children and encourage them to do their best in whatever job they perform

TEACHERS

- Helps instructors to more clearly point out the need for and importance of workers whose jobs require a year or less of preparation
- Provides hope and encouragement to students with disabilities or special needs, at-risk youth, and other individuals who face extraordinary challenges
- Helps provide realistic alternatives for students who will not, cannot, and, in some cases, should not pursue an associate's or bachelor's degree

COUNSELORS

(Includes student support personnel in both public and private settings)

■ Helps counselors more effectively advise students and relate a Good Job selection to a person's life-direction pursuits

■ Helps counselors more realistically guide people who have post-secondary degrees and/or many years of experience to explore Good Jobs or certification as a viable degree- or job-complement option

■ Provides a helpful tool to re-orient other professionals to the value of Good Jobs

■ Provides a valuable supplement to the usual resources, which tend to overlook jobs that require a year or less of preparation

■ Provides a rationale for more employers to adjust their attitudes about the value of and compensation for the work their employees perform

EMPLOYERS

■ Encourages employers to implement a living wage and improve fringe benefits for employees who perform Good Jobs, and to value the work rather than the time spent preparing for the job

■ If employees are aware of the value their job provides to themselves, their employer, and society, and if employers make tangible efforts to show appreciation, it may increase work quality, speed production, and generate worker loyalty

What Will You Find in This Book?

Quick Prep Careers begins with definitions of key terms and phrases in Chapter One. Some terms may be familiar to you, while others, particularly the term Good Jobs, are defined in a new way that considers a larger life picture. Definitions are also provided for Great Jobs and Best Jobs, in order to more clearly distinguish how they differ from Good Jobs. Chapter One also identifies the special population groups that are most likely to benefit from Good Jobs. Among the groups are senior citizens, part-timers/temps, job complement, degree complement, single parents, and others. The chapter concludes with definitions and a discussion of attitudes and their importance in how we perceive Good Jobs.

Chapter Two profiles 50 Good Jobs that require little or no training prior to entry and short-term, on-the-job training after entry.

The phenomenal growth in the quest for certification is the focus of Chapter Three. This chapter profiles 25 careers for which voluntary or required certification either has been recently introduced or has become increasingly popular.

Chapter Four helps you decide if short-term, on-the-job training or certification might be a viable choice for you. The chapter's most important feature is the self-assessment survey provided to help you analyze your values, goals, strengths, weaknesses, and other aspects of your personality and life to determine which job option would be best.

The book concludes with a list of printed and Web site resources and an index.

Career Profiles

Each of the book's 75 career profiles begins with a job title followed by a paragraph that describes major job tasks and responsibilities. Following the job description are several subsections. Here is a summary of what you'll find in each of these subsections.

MAY BE GOOD FOR YOU NOW IF YOU

This section provides a list of reasons why this job may be good for you at this particular time in your life. A job can be good for you during a period of time in your life, and at another time, the same job may be detrimental to your career or life goals. A job that is bad at any time in life for one person can be good throughout life for someone else.

A job is good if it is not self-destructive, helps you move closer to fulfilling your career development goals, and makes a positive contribution to society. All of these characteristics must be present in order for the job to be considered good. Workers are not always conscious of, or do not value, these job characteristics, and it is this reason, in large part, that prompted the writing of this book.

HELPFUL PERSONAL TRAITS

This section highlights a few personal qualities that could improve your chances of success in this job. Qualities cited may include skills, temperaments, strengths, and attitudes. For example:

- Able to inspire productivity and exact loyalty from others
- Able to solve problems
- Punctual and reliable
- Friendly and outgoing
- Aptitude for math

VALUE TO YOUR CAREER DEVELOPMENT

This section lists how the job could supplement other aspects of your most cherished values and personal characteristics. Knowing how a job connects to your deeper meaning and purpose in life can provide motivation and improve work quality. Such knowledge can also help you during times of discouragement and heightened stress. It may also inspire you to select a job that others view as not appropriate or beneficial. (Life values and work values are defined in the Self-Assessment and Profile Sheet. See pages 276-292.)

VALUE TO EMPLOYER/SOCIETY

This section describes the job's value to the employer and its contribution to society. The job should be viewed from a big-picture approach that puts the job in perspective and points to the importance of attitude. It is believed that when you genuinely appreciate the positive impact your job has, it can raise self-esteem, motivation, and a desire to do your best, in spite of some of the job's downsides.

POSSIBLE DOWNSIDES

Information in this section attempts to give a realistic balance to individuals who may be interested in this job. Some of the not-so-pleasant tasks or conditions associated with the job are listed. Some of these characteristics may mean the job is not a good choice for you. However, the information is intended to motivate you to investigate further and then make the appropriate decision.

POPULATION GROUPS

Ten population groups have been identified because it is believed that individuals in these categories could benefit from working in one or more of the 75 jobs included in this book. Of course, the groups are not all-inclusive, and others could most likely be added. The General population group is a catch-all for people who do not fit other population groups. The ten population groups are listed below. Detailed definitions of these groups begin on page 15.

- Part-Time/Temporary
- Single Parent
- Limited Disabled
- Ex-Offender
- Senior Citizen
- Job Complement
- Degree Complement
- Volunteer
- Immigrant/Refugee
- General

PREPARATION

This section provides information about any formal academic preparation or training required to enter this job. Also included is training that may be required after you are hired. For some jobs, suggestions are given regarding preparation that may be helpful for advancement possibilities. Some career profiles state whether certification can enhance prospects for better pay or advancement.

CERTIFICATION

If certification is required or available for the job, it will be cited in this section along with the sponsoring agency. Some jobs are highly regulated and have strict certification and licensing requirements. Many jobs have voluntary certification, which can demonstrate a certain level of skill, training, and commitment. Certification may help you get a job or perhaps help you advance to a higher position with better pay and benefits. There are many more certification opportunities than are listed—some employers have their own training and certification programs; manufacturers sometimes train and certify users of their products; and there may be some local organizations in your area that offer certification. You will probably learn about these types of certification by word-of-mouth as you prepare for and begin to work in your job.

RELATED JOBS/TITLES

This section lists a few of the different names for the same job. Also listed are some closely related jobs that might require similar skills and preparation.

EARNINGS

This section provides a salary range for the job from low to middle to high. Figures come from the U.S. Bureau of Labor Statistics and represent earnings for the year 2000. Ten percent of the employees in this occupation earned the lowest amount or less. The middle figure represents the median earnings for all workers in this occupation. Ten percent of workers earned the highest amount listed or more.

OUTLOOK

The Outlook section summarizes the job in terms of the general economy and industry projections. For the most part, Outlook information is obtained from the U.S. Department of Labor and is supplemented by information taken from professional associations. Job growth terms follow those used in the *Occupational Outlook Handbook:*

■ Growth described as "much faster than the average" means an increase of 36 percent or more

■ Growth described as "faster than the average" means an increase of 21 to 35 percent

■ Growth described as "about as fast as the average" means an increase of 10 to 20 percent

■ Growth described as "little change or more slowly than the average" means an increase of 0 to 9 percent

■ "Decline" means a decrease of 1 percent or more

FOR MORE INFORMATION

This section provides names, addresses, phone numbers, and Web site addresses of organizations that provide more information on the occupation. Wherever possible, we have indicated the type of information each organization offers so that you can better direct your research.

Changing Perceptions

America needs many types and levels of workers. Despite the elimination of numerous jobs due to rapid computerization, millions of people will still be needed to do what some may refer to as mundane, routine, or unattractive jobs. Most of these jobs will require a year or less of training to enter and are often characterized by low pay, few if any fringe benefits, and high turnover.

Unfortunately, too many parents, employers, educators, and media personnel have promoted the bachelor's degree (or advanced degree) as the only acceptable job preparation option. Could it be that this attitude has contributed to the high levels of job-related stress evident in the lives of thousands who work in jobs not considered to be good, great, or the best? Many of these workers are regularly reminded in not-so-subtle ways that they are really not successful. They may feel frustrated, undervalued, and underpaid.

While there may be a few exceptions, most of the jobs in America that require a year or less of preparation, no matter how mundane and seemingly insignificant, have an important and valuable impact. Such jobs can not only be considered good for the worker, but they should be considered by more employers, educators, and parents as vital, necessary, and good.

Quick Prep Careers is meant to be more than a list of jobs that require short-term training or certification. It is intended to help you more accurately decide on the appropriateness of a Good Job or a certification job. Perhaps you will consider one of these jobs a viable option for yourself, whether you are entering the job market for the first time, changing careers, or re-entering the workforce after an absence.

Hopefully this book can assist in encouraging a genuine change in traditional attitudes about Quick Prep jobs, their importance, and future implications. It is important that more people in our society positively recognize, give credit to, and compensate adequately the millions of workers who make it possible for millions of others to live and enjoy their current lifestyles. When this becomes more widespread, then we can expect some real progress.

This book points out that earning certification, in most instances, brings a level of respect, attractiveness, and value, something that is lacking in the majority of Good Jobs, even though both categories require a year or less of preparation. It may be that certification or some other official recognition will one day be required for all of the Good Jobs described here, a trend that could positively impact the viewpoint of many employees, employers, and the public. A changed viewpoint could result in wage and benefit increases where they are painfully low and instill pride in everyone who holds a Good Job.

CHAPTER ONE

GOOD JOBS FOR WHOM? SOME DEFINITIONS

Most of us are familiar with the phrase "Beauty is in the eye of the beholder." The definition of beauty changes with each beholder. Similarly, meanings of terms, such as work, good job, great job, best job, short-term training, certificate, and others are largely dependent on who is doing the defining. This chapter begins with definitions so that there will be little doubt about what is meant by terms and phrases used throughout the book.

Training and Preparation Definitions

SHORT-TERM TRAINING OPTION. This general term refers to jobs for which preparation requirements may be equivalent to, or combine elements from, one or more of the following categories defined by the U.S. Department of Labor. The one common aspect found in each of the categories is that formal preparation requirements for entry usually do not exceed one year.

POSTSECONDARY VOCATIONAL TRAINING. This type of training may lead to a certificate or other award but not a degree. Some postsecondary vocational training programs last only a few weeks, and others may last a year or more. Some occupations may require a licensing examination, which may be included as part of the training program. This type of training may be offered by community, technical, or vocational institutions or bachelor's degree-granting colleges and universities.

WORK EXPERIENCE IN A RELATED OCCUPATION. This term describes occupations that require skills and experience gained in a related occupation or developed from hobbies, non-work activities, or service in the armed forces. Most occupations are supervisory or managerial.

MODERATE-TERM ON-THE-JOB TRAINING. This type of training teaches workers the skills they need during a one- to 12-month period of combined on-the-job experience and informal training sessions.

SHORT-TERM ON-THE-JOB TRAINING. Workers develop skills they need after a short demonstration of job duties and instruction within the first month of employment.

CERTIFICATE. A certificate is an official document often awarded after the successful completion of a training and/or examination program. Some, although not all, of the categories above also will grant a diploma or certificate upon successful completion of a training program.

VIRTUAL OR ONLINE OPTION. Distance-learning courses or programs are offered over the Internet by various agencies, private companies, colleges, and universities.

WORK. Work is effort put forth to accomplish a goal, including physical, emotional, mental, or spiritual effort, or a combination. When applied to an occupation, the objective of work is to provide or produce goods and services for yourself or others.

Job Category Definitions

GOOD JOBS. A Good Job is one that is right, proper, or suitable for an individual at a particular time in his or her life. How good a job is depends on how appropriately it fits your unique personal characteristics and deepest life values. A Good Job for you at a point in time in your life may be a bad job for someone else.

For example, a large number of Good Jobs are part-time positions, often held by teenagers and, to a lesser extent, senior citizens. These groups frequently elect to work part-time because other commitments will not allow them to work full-time hours or they simply cannot find suitable full-time work. A teen who is looking for work experience and a little extra pocket money may find a good part-time position as a cashier at a fast-food restaurant. But that may not be a Good Job for a 30-year-old immigrant man who lacks English speaking skills.

Good Jobs can be found in almost every sector of society, but very few job hunters base their career search on careful and comprehensive scrutiny of personal qualities and values. Too many fall into a job or just take whatever comes along. Others just take the job that pays the most and give little thought to other options. After working with hundreds of career changers over the last 20 years, I have discovered that many people view most, if not all, Good Jobs with disfavor. They see these jobs as having little value and work in them only temporarily until something better comes along. Some people are reluctant to exert anything more than the minimum effort when employed in a job of this type. As a result, work quality suffers, and employers have to contend with high turnover rates.

Good Jobs, in part, are called good because they involve tasks that help you increasingly realize your strongest and most cherished values. That is not to deny the importance of earning an adequate income and receiving benefits, but it must be emphasized that you can be content and satisfied in spite of economic and material success or hardships. When you appreciate and accept the contributory characteristics of a job, as well as its personal complementary nature, then it becomes a Good Job for you.

GREAT JOBS. Great Jobs are highly desired because they provide the employee with a sense of contribution, adequate wages, good fringe benefits, and a relatively secure occupational outlook.

BEST JOBS. Best Jobs are the ones you hear about the most. They are frequently discussed in popular periodicals and in electronic media. Competition for these jobs is often keen, and there are sometimes waiting lists of qualified people seeking employment. These jobs have low turnover rates. Best Jobs usually provide outstanding benefits for their employees, such as:

- Exceptionally high wages
- Generous vacation and holiday plans
- Comprehensive health benefits that include dental, vision, hospitalization, and medical coverage
- Child and elder care
- Wellness and fitness programs
- Life insurance and legal insurance
- Bonuses
- 401-K plans
- Transportation service
- Relocation assistance
- Career development assistance
- College tuition reimbursement programs

Population Group Definitions

Each of the career profiles included in this book has a section called Population Groups, which lists the groups that are likely to derive the most benefit from that job. The lists are not exclusive—there are certainly other groups for whom each job would be appropriate. Following are definitions of the various population groups used in this book.

PART-TIME/TEMPORARY. This population group reflects a wide cross-section of America and includes high school and college students, temporary workers, and senior citizens. With the phenomenal growth of workers employed by temporary agencies, few occupational areas are without temporary workers. A large number of people who work part-time are in the retail, food preparation and service, and education industries. The continuing use of a large number of part-time workers is considered crucial to a significant number of American employers. Hiring part-time workers allows businesses to hold down labor costs, primarily because they do not have to pay full-time fringe benefits. This is particularly important for owners of small businesses.

There are workers in this category who find that the lack of full-time hours and/or fringe benefits presents a financial hardship. These workers may work two part-time jobs, or they may move into better paying, higher benefit, management positions. However, even though part-timers desire higher pay and increased benefits, the majority accept the conditions. Many verbally complain about low wages and yet, if pressed to explain why they stay, they would agree that the job is good for them at this particular time in their lives.

SINGLE PARENT. This population group may include people who have responsibility for one or more children as a result of divorce, death of a spouse, or having children out of wedlock.

There are many Good Jobs for single parents who are on public assistance and need to find work or want to get off welfare. Low-paying, low-benefit jobs may be the only ones available to a single parent who lacks skills (for example, a recently divorced mother who has been out of the workforce for a number of years). Because of their family situations, many single parents find that a Good Job for them right now is a part-time or short-term job that allows them to spend time with their children.

LIMITED DISABLED. This population group is made up of individuals who have some disabilities due to injury or disease. Also included are people with emotional, developmental, and learning disabilities. Some among this group may be able to effectively train for and perform only jobs that require a year or less of preparation. There are, of course, many people with disabilities who can successfully complete bachelor's and advanced degrees and perform jobs as well as anyone with the same education, but without any disabilities. Unfortunately, it is regularly reported that unemployment among the disabled is especially high. There appears to be a continuing reluctance among employers to hire individuals with disabilities. Because of the lack of acceptance of people in this population group, they may feel they are contributing less or performing tasks considered less important. Educators and employers must emphasize the value of the contribution of people with disabilities, and they must communicate this idea not only to those with disabilities, but to everyone.

EX-OFFENDER. Many in this population group may view Good Jobs as stepping stones to other occupations. Some may see Good Jobs as safe, nonthreatening experiences that help them to re-establish a sense of responsibility. Such jobs may serve to convince employers, family members, or friends that they can be trusted and are ready for advancement. Others within this group determine that a Good Job experience is suitable for them at this stage of their life to build self-confidence, establish a work history, or confront fears of failure.

SENIOR CITIZEN. Many senior citizens work part-time and at or near minimum-wage levels. Good Jobs may be just right for those who have already completed years of full-time paid work in the past but aren't quite ready to leave the workforce. Good Jobs can provide personal fulfillment as well as an important financial supplement after retirement. In some situations, seniors who work with high school and college-age co-workers (which is becoming more commonplace in many fast-food establishments) have opportunities to share their years of life experiences. Younger workers and employers, as well as the seniors themselves, benefit from such working relationships. In addition to the contact with younger people and the opportunity to render a valuable social service, the extra cash can provide an economic boost to a set pension.

JOB COMPLEMENT. Individuals in this population group already hold a full-time job. They usually enter certification programs to either enhance their chances for advancement in their current work setting or to improve their competitive edge, should they decide to leave their current job. Some in this group may not have formal education beyond high school but have acquired a great deal of on-the-job experience and know-how. Others may have acquired an associate's, bachelor's, or even a master's degree. After completing a certificate program, these workers have official documentation that they have acquired specific skills or training, which is likely to earn them higher pay, expanded benefits, and an increased sense of fulfillment.

DEGREE COMPLEMENT. This population group is made up of those who possess a bachelor's degree or higher and elect to pursue certification for one or more reasons. Some may have majored in liberal arts subjects and experienced difficulty finding employment. Some may have retired from previous full-time occupations and decided to re-enter the labor force in a different area from their previous career focus; they need to upgrade or add new expertise or technical skills in order to increase their marketability. Some want to learn specific skills that will complement their current job or degree in hopes of improving their competitive position or opening the door for advancement.

VOLUNTEER. Volunteering, or engaging in purposeful activity for the benefit of others without receiving or seeking monetary compensation, has gained in popularity in recent years. It is something that people of all ages and economic, educational, and ethnic backgrounds can successfully engage in. High school and college students, in particular, are discovering that volunteering can provide immense satisfaction and help them experience a more fulfilling life, as well as help to meet a vital need in communities all across the country. More high schools and colleges are granting credit for such involvements and, in addition, volunteer jobs are increasingly seen as valued work experience by employers. Some volunteer involvements can lead to job offers.

IMMIGRANT/REFUGEE. Individuals in this group are recent newcomers from another country. Immigrants usually leave their country voluntarily and often come to America to join family, increase their income, or improve their overall quality of life. Some may have few or no transferable skills. Consequently, they may be willing to work in less-than-desirable, low-income, low-benefit jobs. Sometimes a number of immigrants from the same foreign country or community share housing, pool their income, and eventually save enough to buy their own properties.

Other immigrants have a business background or professional experience and can apply their expertise in American jobs. Some professions require immigrants to have additional training or certification to comply with American standards.

There are also refugees that come to America to escape persecution, famine, war, or another disaster that makes it impossible for them to remain in their homeland. They face significant challenges once they arrive, one of which is finding work. Many in this population group are likely be appreciative of any employment possibility. For them, minimum-wage, low-benefit, and even unpleasant jobs are Good Jobs.

Many businesses depend on this population group for their survival. Immigrants and refugees provide a valuable contribution to the workforce and at the same time are provided with Good Jobs that can help them make the transition to the American way of life.

GENERAL. Individuals in this population group do not clearly fall into any of the other groups listed. Following are some of the special subgroups included in the General category. When General is listed on a career profile, it could apply to one or more of these categories:

A. Single individuals who have never been married or are divorced with no dependents. Some in this subgroup have few if any marketable skills, but otherwise they have no disabilities.

B. Adults who have never worked but want to find suitable employment that will either supplement the family income or provide personal fulfillment without dedicating long years to training and education. This subgroup includes mothers who may have dedicated 15 to 20 years to raising children and managing a household and have never worked outside of the home for wages. They are now preparing to return or have returned to school in an effort to acquire marketable skills that can be applied to jobs they consider good for them at this time in life.

C. Part-time or full-time college students.

D. Individuals who are unhappy with their current employment situation or have burned themselves out on their last job and want to make a career change without years of preparation.

E. Others who are not mentioned but do not clearly fit any of the other population groups or subgroups described.

Attitudes

There is a need for a change in the generally unsupportive attitudes about Good Jobs in American society. I have listened to or read comments from employees expressing negativity about their Good Jobs. I have often had clients make statements that show they place little value on Good Jobs. Before I share some examples of these attitudes, it's necessary to define what I mean by positive and negative attitudes.

WHAT IS AN ATTITUDE?

An attitude is a way of thinking and feeling about something, someone, or some situation. Attitudes are often made apparent to others through behavior, speech, body language, and facial expression. What you think and feel inside, in large part, is based on your past experiences, which have significantly influenced who you are right now.

WHAT IS A POSITIVE ATTITUDE?

A positive attitude can be defined as a favorable way of thinking and feeling. People with positive attitudes are frequently described as:

Optimistic	Cheerful	Grateful
Prompt	Pleasant	Helpful
Hopeful	Tactful	Willing
Kind	Respectful	Cooperative
Polite	Dependable	Neat
Sensitive	Supportive	Friendly

The regular practice of positive attitudes can improve your chances of having a fulfilling career, increase the likelihood of realizing personal life values at a higher intensity, and encourage others in their pursuits.

WHAT IS A NEGATIVE ATTITUDE?

A negative attitude can be defined as a self-defeating and unfavorable way of thinking and feeling. People with negative attitudes are often described as:

Cocky	Hostile	Pessimistic
Irresponsible	Belligerent	Apathetic
Critical	Unwilling	Doubtful
Fearful	Aggressive	Hopeless
Flippant	Argumentative	Hateful
Nonchalant	Distrustful	Rude
Unmotivated	Lazy	Confrontational
Disrespectful	Sarcastic	Condescending
Unsupportive	Impatient	Insensitive

The regular practice of negative attitudes can hamper your chances of having a fulfilling career, stall your personal achievements, and discourage others in their pursuits.

Too many parents, employers, and employees themselves hold negative attitudes about Good Jobs, which may perpetuate self-defeating behaviors. For example, an employer who is consistently unsupportive, condescending, and unwilling to accept a slightly lower profit margin to better ensure that employees earn a living wage and reasonable benefits would be demonstrating a negative attitude. A parent who looks down on Good Jobs and refuses to financially support a son or daughter's decision to become employed in a Good Job is displaying and perpetuating a negative attitude. Here are some comments from workers that show negative attitudes about Good Jobs:

"This job sucks, and I'm not going to break my neck when I only get minimum wage."

"This job ain't about nothing!"

"Why don't you get a REAL job?"

"I'll work anywhere, even if it's at a fast-food joint!"

"I'm just a janitor." (Or a maid or garbage collector, etc.)

"I don't like to tell people where I work because it's kind of embarrassing."

"I don't care about this job because I plan to quit pretty soon."

"I'm just waiting tables right now."

OBSERVATIONS

Following are some specific examples, along with some observations and questions about prevalent attitudes toward Good Jobs in American society.

OBSERVATION 1. A middle-aged man expressed his frustration about not being able to find a job. He had a master's degree in computers and had worked for many years in the field before his employer downsized and he was laid off. His job-hunting efforts had come to a stall, and he was desperate. His bills were stacking up, and he said he would be willing to work at almost any job, even a low-paying, fast-food job. Unfortunately, managers were reluctant to hire him for these types of jobs. The man felt this was because the managers assumed he would leave as soon as a better, higher-paying job opened up. But for this man, at this time in his life, a Good Job would be most appropriate.

Most of us would probably have a similar attitude, should hardship or disaster enter into our lives and shake us from our Great Jobs. Does it take something like this man's experience for people to see the value of Good Jobs? If so, will the changed attitude toward Good Jobs last only until a better job comes along, or will the experience bring about a new, lasting appreciation for the value of Good Jobs?

OBSERVATION 2. A young man who had been in this country for a short period of time shared with me that he had earned a college degree prior to coming to America, but most of his credits did not transfer. He had gone back to school and earned a degree in business. After looking for a job, he became discouraged and eventually quit searching. I asked about his current employment situation, and he said he was working full-time at a local factory. His gestures, body language, and facial expressions led me to believe that he thought the job was beneath him, and he expressed clear disdain.

I quickly lost patience with this young man because I had recently been working with so many who were out of work and would have been pleased to have his factory job. My attempts to get him to see the value of having a job and the possible benefits were not too successful. Later I realized I may have been insensitive. There are thousands of people who hold college degrees—some born in this country, some not—who have to, or choose to, work in Good Jobs to survive financially. For these people, negative attitudes perhaps are understandable. Wouldn't anyone in that situation demonstrate a similar attitude? However, there are some important questions to ask that might put Good Jobs in perspective and change those negative attitudes. What if there were no Good Jobs available to fall back on? Aren't Good Jobs as important as Great Jobs in terms of their contribution to the entire employment picture in this country? Does a negative attitude affect the quality of your work? If so, how does your negative attitude affect the attitudes and work of co-workers who do not hold a degree and have no hopes or intentions of moving into a Great Job?

OBSERVATION 3. A refugee who had been hired as a hand packer by one of our local food stores was one of a number who had left their country in fear for their lives. Some of them had never in their lives worked at a job for pay. This refugee had been working only a short time, but he had already developed an unfavorable attitude toward Good Jobs. When I asked him about his job as a packer, his response was not one that communicated gratitude or optimism. He was frustrated that he did not have one of the better jobs that others had at the store. Could he have been influenced by the Americans he worked with and picked up on their negative attitudes? Could he have heard great things about opportunities in America, set unrealistically high expectations, and been disappointed? I do not mean to suggest that anyone should be content with low pay or drudgery or long hours. However, facing those kinds of issues with negativity affects work quality and only serves to feed and sustain the notions that Good Jobs are undesirable, boring, and of little value.

IN CONCLUSION. Jobs that require a year or less of preparation to enter may be the key to America's continuing economic health. Without workers who are currently employed in Good Jobs, the quality of life for millions of Americans would be drastically reduced. Few jobs in America can be considered unimportant or not valuable.

CHAPTER TWO

SHORT-TERM JOB TRAINING: 50 GOOD JOBS

Good Jobs fall in the short-term job training category. They usually require one year or less of preparation. This chapter includes career profiles of 50 Good Jobs.

■ Amusement Recreation Attendant

An amusement recreation attendant may perform a variety of tasks that differ depending on the amusement park, recreational facility, carnival, or rides. Duties may include preparing people for rides, collecting fees, operating rides, instructing people on how to play a game, operating and/or monitoring game, working a concession stand, distributing and picking up equipment, and providing assistance to participants.

MAY BE GOOD FOR YOU NOW IF YOU

- Need and want to make some extra money while in high school or college
- Desire part-time, temporary, or seasonal work only
- Have worked in a circus and/or carnival in the past
- Enjoy working outdoors

HELPFUL PERSONAL TRAITS

- Like working with people who are having fun
- Outgoing
- Friendly
- Adventuresome
- Good customer-relations skills

VALUE TO YOUR CAREER DEVELOPMENT

- Can help meet the values of pleasure and adventure
- Can derive satisfaction from helping others have fun, particularly children

VALUE TO EMPLOYER/SOCIETY

- Helps provide relief from the normal routine for millions each year in the form of pleasure and adventure
- Provides a popular recreational option for many young people

POSSIBLE DOWNSIDES
- Exposed to dangers of a ride-related injury
- Low pay and benefits
- May require long hours in one position or on your feet
- May have to do lifting and climbing

POPULATION GROUPS
- Part-Time/Temporary
- Immigrant/Refugee
- Volunteer
- General

PREPARATION
- A high school diploma is not usually required
- Employer provides on-the-job training

CERTIFICATION
- Certification is not usually associated with this occupation

RELATED JOBS/TITLES
- Recreation Worker
- Carnival Worker

EARNINGS
- $11,610 to $13,980 to $21,380

OUTLOOK
- According to the *Occupational Outlook Handbook,* jobs for amusement recreation attendants are projected to increase much faster than the average through 2010. Most jobs will be for seasonal, full-time work. Many countries abroad are now constructing amusement parks, so job opportunities will also exist outside of the United States.

FOR MORE INFORMATION

For information on the industry and job opportunities, contact:

**International Association of Amusement Parks and
Attractions**
1448 Duke Street
Alexandria, VA 22314-3664
703-836-4800
iaapa@iaapa.org
http://www.iaapa.org

*For information on the history of amusement parks and attractions,
industry publications, conventions, and membership information,
contact:*

National Amusement Park Historical Association
PO Box 83
Mt. Prospect, IL 60056
412-831-6315
http://www.napha.org

*For information on the recreation industry and career opportunities,
contact:*

National Recreation and Park Association
22377 Belmont Ridge Road
Ashburn, VA 20148-4501
703-858-0784
info@nrpa.org
http://www.nrpa.org

*For a list of amusement and theme parks in the United States, or for
historical facts on the industry, contact:*

FunGuide
http://www.funguide.com

For information on career and internship opportunities, contact:

Six Flags Theme Parks
http://www.sixflags.com/Jobs

*For career information, employment opportunities, audition schedules,
or to submit a resume electronically, contact:*

The Walt Disney Company
http://www.disney.com/DisneyCareers

■ Auto Body Repairer

An auto body repairer straightens, removes dents, and replaces parts on vehicles of all types, but particularly automobiles. Duties include identifying appropriate materials to use; soldering; filling; sanding; cleaning surfaces; painting; operating hydraulic jacks; pulling out dents; hammering; replacing parts; using restoration equipment; chaining or clamping frames/sections to alignment machines; reading, understanding, and applying repairs according to specifications; removing damaged sections; and welding.

MAY BE GOOD FOR YOU NOW IF YOU

- Have worked on auto restoration/body work in the past
- Don't mind getting dirty and doing strenuous work

HELPFUL PERSONAL TRAITS

- Hands-on person
- Like challenge of repairing damaged things
- Basic reading and math skills and spatial perception
- Computer-proficient
- Good at understanding technical manuals and following directions

VALUE TO YOUR CAREER DEVELOPMENT

- Can help to meet values of skill, achievement, and physical appearance
- Satisfaction derived from restoring a damaged vehicle to its original appearance

VALUE TO EMPLOYER/SOCIETY

- Helps many people retain a previously damaged vehicle, and thus save the expense of purchasing another vehicle
- Can contribute to the emotional well-being of people who have had bad experiences with car repair
- May prevent future accidents and injuries that may have occurred due to driving damaged vehicles

POSSIBLE DOWNSIDES
- Dirty
- Exposure to fumes from dust and chemicals
- Noisy
- At risk for cuts and burns
- May need to stand and bend a lot and work in awkward positions

POPULATION GROUPS
- Part-Time/Temporary
- General

PREPARATION
- Most employers prefer formal training that can be obtained at the high school or postsecondary school level. Continued training is recommended to acquire a higher skill level and a competitive edge. On-the-job training supplemented by short-term training experiences should be expected after entry.

CERTIFICATION
- Entry-level technicians in the industry can demonstrate their qualifications through certification by the National Automotive Technicians Education Foundation (NATEF), an affiliate of the National Institute for Automotive Service Excellence (ASE). Certification is voluntary. Many trade and vocational schools throughout the country have affiliation with NATEF.

RELATED JOBS/TITLES
- Automotive Painter
- Automotive Glass Installer
- Automotive Service Technician

EARNINGS
- $17,659 to $31,200 to $54,205+

OUTLOOK
- The auto repair industry is facing a labor shortage of skilled entry-level workers in many areas of the country. Demand for collision repair services is expected to remain consistent, and

employment opportunities are expected to increase about as fast as the average through 2010.

FOR MORE INFORMATION

For more information on careers, training, and accreditation, contact the following organizations:

Automotive Aftermarket Industry Association
4600 East-West Highway, Suite 300
Bethesda, MD 20814-3415
301-654-6664
aaia@aftermarket.org
http://www.aftermarket.org

Inter-Industry Conference on Auto Collision Repair
3701 Algonquin Road, Suite 400
Rolling Meadows, IL 60008
800-422-7872
http://www.i-car.com

National Automotive Technicians Education Foundation
101 Blue Seal Drive, Suite 101
Leesburg, VA 20175
703-669-6650
http://www.natef.org

National Institute for Automotive Service Excellence
101 Blue Seal Drive, SE, Suite 101
Leesburg, VA 20175
877-273-8324
http://www.asecert.org

■ Baker

Bakers mix and bake ingredients in accordance with recipes to produce breads, pastries, and other baked goods. A baker may work in a grocery store, specialty shop, or manufacturing firm. Duties include measuring and weighing ingredients, mixing, kneading dough, baking, icing, cake decorating, reading recipes, following instructions, and cleaning equipment. Some bakers serve customers.

MAY BE GOOD FOR YOU NOW IF YOU

- Love to bake at home, are good at it, and want to do it full-time
- Have worked as a cook in the past
- Want to volunteer in this area

HELPFUL PERSONAL TRAITS

- Creative
- Tend to be clean and neat
- Detail-oriented
- Good eye-hand coordination
- Good personal hygiene habits

VALUE TO YOUR CAREER DEVELOPMENT

- May help to meet the values of skill, creativity, recognition, achievement, and knowledge
- Satisfaction derived from appreciation expressed by others for what you have baked

VALUE TO EMPLOYER/SOCIETY

- Provides pleasure for countless people who enjoy pastry and baked goods
- Contributes to making the supply of bread, a staple of the American diet

POSSIBLE DOWNSIDES

- Usually hot and noisy
- Must stand for long periods
- Risk of suffering burns, cuts, and other kitchen-related injuries
- Pressure to meet deadlines

- May work irregular hours
- Low wages

POPULATION GROUPS
- Part-Time/Temporary
- General

PREPARATION
- No formal training required

CERTIFICATION
- The American Institute of Baking offers courses leading to certi-fication in a number of areas: Certified Baker—Bread and Rolls, Certified Baker—Cookies and Crackers, and Certified Maintenance Technician. Some employers may require certifica-tion; in other cases, certification is recommended for those wanting to advance their careers.

RELATED JOBS/TITLES
- Cook
- Pastry Chef
- Food Preparation Worker
- Cake Decorator

EARNINGS
- $13,170 to $19,710 to $31,720

OUTLOOK
- Overall, the U.S. Department of Labor predicts slower-than-average growth through 2010 for all bakery workers. However, there may be a slight increase in the need for bakers at retail locations because of the growing number of traditional bakeries and specialty shops, such as cookie, muffin, and bagel shops.

FOR MORE INFORMATION

For industry information, including salary surveys, contact:

American Bakers Association
1350 I Street, NW, Suite 1290
Washington, DC 20005-3300
202-789-0300
info@americanbakers.org
http://www.americanbakers.org

For information on scholarships, online courses, and employment opportunities, contact:

American Institute of Baking
1213 Bakers Way
PO Box 3999
Manhattan, KS 66505-3999
800-633-5137
info@aibonline.org
http://www.aibonline.org

This organization has industry information for the public and career information available to members.

American Society of Baking
1200 Central Avenue, Suite 360
Wilmette, IL 60091
866-920-9885
http://www.asbe.org

This organization provides opportunities for the interaction and exchange of information among bakers, their suppliers, and specialists in the science of baking and baking ingredients.

The Bread Bakers Guild of America
3203 Maryland Avenue
North Versailles, PA 15137
412-322-8275
http://www.bbga.org

■ Bill Collector

A bill collector maintains records and overdue accounts and implements strategies to collect payments from customers who are delinquent. Some work for third parties, while others are employees of creditor organizations (stores, hospitals, etc.). Duties may include assisting customers with arrangements for paying their bills, locating and notifying customers of overdue accounts, and collecting payment. Other tasks may include initiating repossession proceedings, service discontinuation, or referral for legal action.

MAY BE GOOD FOR YOU NOW IF YOU

- Can relate to those who may have difficulty keeping commitments and believe your people skills can lead to successful collections
- Desire to do volunteer work in this area

HELPFUL PERSONAL TRAITS

- Good negotiating and persuasive skills
- Persistent
- Able to sensitively interact with people of different backgrounds in a variety of situations
- Can accept criticism and maintain composure in stressful situations
- Patient, discreet, and tactful
- Excellent telephone skills

VALUE TO YOUR CAREER DEVELOPMENT

- Can help meet the values of justice and helping others
- Can increase sensitivity toward those who do not pay bills as promised
- Satisfaction derived from helping others keep commitments, become debt-free, and possibly live a more responsible life

VALUE TO EMPLOYER/SOCIETY

- Helps employers improve their bottom-line percentages and hopefully minimize the possibility of the cost of noncollection being passed on through higher prices

■ In cases where loan delinquencies are especially high, successful bill collectors may be the key to a company's survival

POSSIBLE DOWNSIDES

■ May frequently be confronted by angry customers

■ Deadline pressures

■ May not receive recognition for successes

■ Most contacts with customers are usually under unpleasant circumstances

POPULATION GROUPS

■ Part-Time/Temporary

■ Volunteer

■ General

PREPARATION

■ No formal training is required usually

■ On-the-job training is normally offered through the employer

■ Experience as a telemarketer may be helpful

CERTIFICATION

■ Although it is not required by law, some employers require their employees to become certified by the American Collectors Association (ACA). The ACA conducts seminars on state and federal compliance laws that pertain to collection workers.

RELATED JOBS/TITLES

■ Collector

■ Collection Specialist

■ Collection Manager

■ Compliance Officer

■ Insurance Adjuster Investigator

■ Credit Manager

EARNINGS

■ $15,900 to $23,540 to $34,800

OUTLOOK

■ Employment for bill collectors is predicted by the U.S. Department of Labor to grow faster than the average through 2010. The department also notes that hospitals and physicians' offices are two of the fastest-growing employers of bill collectors and collection agencies.

FOR MORE INFORMATION

For a brochure on careers in collection work, contact:

ACA International
Association of Credit and Collection Professionals
PO Box 390106
Minneapolis, MN 55439
952-926-6547
http://www.collector.com

For information on careers and certification, contact NACM:

National Association of Credit Management (NACM)
8840 Columbia 100 Parkway
Columbia, MD 21045
410-740-5560
nacm_info@nacm.org
http://www.nacm.org

■ Building Cleaning Worker

A building cleaning worker may do the same work as a janitor, maid, or housekeeper. Duties vary depending on location but may include all or most of the following: cleaning floors and vacuuming rugs, washing walls, cleaning inside windows, emptying trash containers, dusting and polishing furniture, straightening and rearranging furniture, disinfecting and sterilizing equipment, and cleaning ovens and refrigerators. Maids and housekeepers may also clean toilets, replenish bathroom supplies, change and make beds, fold and iron laundry, wash dishes, run errands, and do record keeping.

MAY BE GOOD FOR YOU NOW IF YOU

■ Want to work part-time

■ Have limited skills or work experience

■ Enjoy cleaning up

■ Have cleaned buildings or homes in the past

HELPFUL PERSONAL TRAITS

■ Industrious

■ Able to work without direct supervision as well as with a team

■ Good at understanding and following instructions

■ Friendly and conscientious

■ Responsible and trustworthy

VALUE TO YOUR CAREER DEVELOPMENT

■ May help meet the values of health, organization, safety, physical appearance, and achievement

■ Satisfaction derived from having provided others with a clean, safe environment

VALUE TO EMPLOYER/SOCIETY

■ Contributes to a building's attractiveness and appeal to visitors, patrons, residents, and buyers

■ Can prevent injuries and possibly illnesses due to unkempt, dirty, or dangerous areas in buildings

POSSIBLE DOWNSIDES
- Low pay and benefits
- May have to work evenings, nights, weekends, and holidays
- Must stand for long periods
- Lifting, bending, and stooping may increase risk of back injury
- Can be dirty and unpleasant

POPULATION GROUPS
- Part-Time/Temporary
- General
- Immigrant/Refugee
- Limited Disabled

PREPARATION
- No prior formal education or experience is necessary
- Tasks are usually learned on the job
- A high school diploma may improve chances for advancement

CERTIFICATION
- Certification is not usually associated with this occupation, but certification in housekeeping is available from the National Executive Housekeepers Association (NEHA). The NEHA offers two levels of certification, which indicate a certain degree of professionalism and training and may be beneficial in finding a job or in moving to a better position.

RELATED JOBS/TITLES
- Maid
- Cleaner
- Housekeeping Cleaner
- Housekeeper
- Custodian
- Janitor

EARNINGS
- Cleaners and janitors: $12,280 to $17,180 to $29,190
- Maids and housekeepers: $11,910 to $15,810 to $22,200

OUTLOOK

■ Employment for this occupation is expected to grow as fast as the average through 2010, according to the U.S. Department of Labor. Businesses providing janitorial and cleaning services on a contract basis are expected to be among the fastest-growing employers of these workers.

FOR MORE INFORMATION

For information on careers and training in the janitorial services field, contact:

Cleaning and Maintenance Management Online
National Trade Publications
13 Century Hill Drive
Latham, NY 12110
518-783-1281
http://www.cmmonline.com

For information about certification programs in housekeeping, contact:

International Executive Housekeepers Association, Inc.
1001 Eastwind Drive, Suite 301
Westerville, OH 43081-3361
800-200-6342
excel@ieha.org
http://www.ieha.org

■ Bus Driver

A bus driver drives passengers on a bus to and from destinations following a predetermined schedule and route. The route could be intercity, within a region, or across the country. Tasks can include picking up and dropping off passengers, collecting fees (tickets or money), passing out transfer slips and bus schedules, and selling bus tickets. In addition, bus drivers maintain order, enforce regulations and safety rules, conduct safety checks, respond to inquiries, announce stops, and complete reports.

MAY BE GOOD FOR YOU NOW IF YOU
- Are good at handling/operating large vehicles
- Enjoy challenges
- Have driven a bus or truck
- Enjoy working around people
- Desire to work part-time or on a temporary basis

HELPFUL PERSONAL TRAITS
- Able to manage large groups of people
- Good vision, color perception, and eye-hand-foot coordination
- Able to work with people from differing backgrounds and ethnicities
- Able to react quickly, work under pressure, and meet deadlines
- Responsible and alert
- Patient
- Manual dexterity

VALUE TO YOUR CAREER DEVELOPMENT
- May help to meet the values of power, skill, helping others, and achievement
- Satisfaction derived from knowing you have provided a valuable service for your riders

VALUE TO EMPLOYER/SOCIETY
- Provides a primary source of transportation for the large number of people who travel daily to and from work or school

POSSIBLE DOWNSIDES
- Driving in bad weather
- Possibility of having an accident
- Can experience stress due to unruly and/or uncooperative passengers
- Some may work long hours, while others don't get enough hours

POPULATION GROUPS
- Part-Time/Temporary
- Single Parent
- General

PREPARATION
- Should be a high school graduate and have a good driving record
- Must meet qualifications set by state and federal regulations
- Must obtain a commercial driver's license (CDC)
- Most states require you to be 21 or older
- Will probably have to take a drug test

CERTIFICATION
- Certification is not usually associated with this occupation

RELATED JOBS/TITLES
- Truck Driver
- Taxi Driver
- Chauffeur
- Subway Train Driver
- Ambulance Driver

EARNINGS
- Transit/intercity bus drivers: $15,890 to $25,710 to $41,660
- School bus drivers: $12,460 to $20,910 to $32,200

OUTLOOK
- According to the *Occupational Outlook Handbook,* jobs for bus drivers are projected to increase about as fast as the average through 2010. Future government efforts to reduce traffic and

pollution through greater funding of public transportation could greatly improve job opportunities. Because many bus driver positions offer relatively high wages and attractive benefits, job seekers may face heavy competition. Those who have good driving records and are willing to work in rapidly growing metropolitan areas will have the best opportunities.

FOR MORE INFORMATION

For transit news and links to local chapters, contact:

Amalgamated Transit Union
5025 Wisconsin Avenue, NW
Washington, DC 20016-4139
202-537-1645
http://www.atu.org

For information on the intercity bus industry, contact:

American Bus Association
1100 New York Avenue, NW, Suite 1050
Washington, DC 20005
http://www.buses.org

For salary statistics and other career information, contact:

American Public Transit Association
1666 K Street, NW
Washington, DC 20006
202-496-4889
http://www.apta.com

For information on careers in public transportation, contact:

Transport Workers Union of America
80 West End Avenue
New York, NY 10023
212-873-6000
http://www.twu.com

For information on school bus contractors, contact:

National School Transportation Association
625 Slaters Lane, Suite 205
Alexandria, VA 22314
http://www.schooltrans.com

■ Cashier

A cashier serves customers by totaling the amount owed for merchandise or service to be purchased, receiving money, and making and returning appropriate change when necessary. Other duties may include maintaining familiarity with policies and sales; answering customer inquiries; handling returns and exchanges; receiving, verifying, and obtaining authorization of identification information; and counting and balancing money in the drawer before and after work. Some may calculate and organize coupons, returns, and exchanges, as well as bag and wrap items.

MAY BE GOOD FOR YOU NOW IF YOU
- Want to work part-time, temporarily, evenings, or weekends
- Like to work with the public
- Plan to eventually have a full-time career in the retail industry

HELPFUL PERSONAL TRAITS
- Strong numerical skills
- Accurate, detail-oriented, and efficient
- Good with money
- Responsible and possess a high degree of integrity
- Polite
- Good people skills

VALUE TO YOUR CAREER DEVELOPMENT
- May help meet the values of skill, helping others, achievement, and recognition
- Satisfaction derived from knowing you are being efficient and responsible in handling money and serving people

VALUE TO EMPLOYER/SOCIETY
- Efficient performance along with a pleasant attitude can contribute to customer satisfaction, which maintains or increases patronage and revenues

POSSIBLE DOWNSIDES
- Must stand for long periods
- Can be repetitive

■ May be more vulnerable to criminal activity as a result of working around large amounts of cash

POPULATION GROUPS
■ Part-Time/Temporary

■ Single Parent

■ Senior Citizen

■ General

PREPARATION
■ Although not required, a high school diploma is usually preferred

■ Training is normally conducted by the employer

■ Previous business, computer, or sales experience is helpful

CERTIFICATION
■ Certification is not usually associated with this occupation

RELATED JOBS/TITLES
■ Bank Teller

■ Counter Clerk

■ Retail Salesperson

■ Rental Clerk

■ Food Service Worker

EARNINGS
■ $11,670 to $14,460 to $21,610+

OUTLOOK
■ According to the *Occupational Outlook Handbook,* jobs for cashiers are projected to grow about as fast as the average through 2010. Due to a high turnover rate among cashiers, many jobs will become available as workers leaving the field are replaced. Each year almost one-third of all cashiers leave their jobs for various reasons.

   Many part-time jobs should be available. Although the majority of cashiers employed are 24 years of age or younger, many businesses have started diversifying their workforce by hiring older persons and those with disabilities to fill some job openings. Future job opportunities will be available to those experienced in bookkeeping, typing, business machine operation, and general office skills.

FOR MORE INFORMATION

For career information, contact:

National Association of Convenience Stores
1605 King Street
Alexandria, VA 22314
http://www.cstorecentral.com

For information about educational programs in the retail industry, contact:

National Retail Federation
325 Seventh Street, NW, Suite 1100
Washington, DC 20004
800-NRF-HOW2
http://www.nrf.com

The UFCW represents workers in retail food, meatpacking, poultry, and other food processing industries. For more information, contact:

United Food and Commercial Workers
International Union (UFCW)
1775 K Street, NW
Washington, DC 20006
202-223-3111
http://www.ufcw.org

■ Child Care Worker

A child care worker watches over, nurtures, and cares for children in the child's home, in a day care facility, or in the home of the child care worker. Duties may include most or all of the following: organizing and implementing play activities, preparing meals, conducting physical exercises, planning and leading educational experiences, teaching and modeling positive character qualities, exercising discipline, and scheduling. Child care workers use strategies and techniques, such as arts and crafts, music, dance, outdoor activities, and trips. Some work as live-in nannies. Child care workers who work in day care centers usually have more structured programs. They may work with teachers and other professionals to develop appropriate activities for large groups children of different ages and needs.

MAY BE GOOD FOR YOU NOW IF YOU
■ Love working with children
■ Have lots of experience raising or caring for children
■ Want to work part-time and/or evenings and weekends
■ Desire to become self-employed
■ Want to work at home

HELPFUL PERSONAL TRAITS
■ Warm and compassionate
■ Kind and gentle
■ Patient
■ Able to understand the needs of preschool-aged children in all stages of development
■ Good verbal skills
■ Creative
■ Enthusiastic
■ Physical endurance
■ Good sense of humor

VALUE TO YOUR CAREER DEVELOPMENT
■ Can help meet the values of love and helping and serving others

- Satisfaction derived from knowing your efforts make a tremendous impact on the lives of young children during their formative years
- Can provide valuable preparation for a career in child care or teaching, or if you are planning to have a family

VALUE TO EMPLOYER/SOCIETY

- Gives many parents a sense of assurance and peace of mind knowing their child is in a safe and wholesome environment during their absence
- Enables millions to hold jobs
- Often considered critical to the nation's working families and employers

POSSIBLE DOWNSIDES

- Low pay and benefits
- Often stressful
- Lack of appreciation for performing a job that has such significant impact on the development of human lives
- May have to work extended hours at times

POPULATION GROUPS

- Part-Time/Temporary
- Single Parent
- Volunteer
- General

PREPARATION

- No formal education required, although a high school diploma is suggested
- To operate as a child care provider, a license is usually required as well as a safety inspection and criminal background check

CERTIFICATION

- Each state sets its own licensing requirements for child care workers. Some states require that you complete a certain number of continuing education hours every year; these hours may include college courses or research into the subject of child care. CPR training is also often required.

National certification isn't required of child care workers, but some organizations do offer it. The Council for Professional Recognition offers the Child Development Associate (CDA) National Credentialing Program. The National Child Care Association offers the Certified Childcare Professional (CCP) Credential.

RELATED JOBS/TITLES
- Family Child Care Provider
- Nanny
- Preschool Assistant
- Kindergarten Teacher
- Teacher Assistant

EARNINGS
- $11,810 to $15,460 to $22,270

OUTLOOK
- According to the *Occupational Outlook Handbook,* jobs for child care workers are projected to increase about as fast as the average through 2010. There is high turnover in this field, resulting in the need for many replacement workers. One reason for this turnover rate is the low pay. Jobs will also be available as more child care centers, both nonprofit and for-profit, open to meet the increased demand for child care. There will be more franchises and national chains offering job opportunities to child care workers, as well as centers that cater exclusively to corporate employees. Child care workers may be working with older children, as more day care centers expand to include elementary school services. Bilingual child care workers will find more job opportunities and better salaries.

FOR MORE INFORMATION
For information about certification, contact:

Council for Professional Recognition
2460 16th Street, NW
Washington, DC 20009-3575
800-424-4310
http://www.cdacouncil.org

For information about student memberships and training opportunities, contact:

National Association of Child Care Professionals
PO Box 90723
Austin, TX 78709-0723
800-537-1118
admin@naccp.org
http://www.naccp.org

For information about certification and to learn about the issues affecting child care, visit the NCCA Web page, or contact:

National Child Care Association (NCCA)
1016 Rosser Street
Conyers, GA 30012
800-543-7161
http://www.nccanet.org

■ Cook

A cook prepares meals for restaurants and institutions, such as schools, hospitals, military establishments, and prisons. Duties may include most or all of the following: measuring, mixing, and cooking ingredients; understanding and following menus and recipes; grilling; preparing sandwiches; frying; planning menus; buying supplies; cleaning, peeling, and slicing vegetables and fruits; and directing other workers.

MAY BE GOOD FOR YOU NOW IF YOU
- Want to work evenings, weekends, or holidays
- Love to cook and have catered or cooked for large groups in the past
- Plan to become a chef

HELPFUL PERSONAL TRAITS
- Creative
- Good health and personal hygiene
- A team player
- Interpersonal communication skills
- Good sense of taste and smell

VALUE TO YOUR CAREER DEVELOPMENT
- Can help meet the values of pleasure, creativity, serving others, and recognition
- Satisfaction derived from customer appreciation for well-prepared and delicious meals

VALUE TO EMPLOYER/SOCIETY
- High-quality, tasty food is considered the lifeline of most eating establishments and therefore key to their survival
- Contributes to the pleasure of dining out, which is an important part of the American way of life

POSSIBLE DOWNSIDES
- Must stand for long periods
- Must lift heavy pots and pans
- Danger of suffering burns, cuts, bruises, and falls
- Low pay

POPULATION GROUPS
- Part-Time/Temporary
- Single Parent
- Limited Disabled
- Volunteer

PREPARATION
- Requires little or no education, but a background in food preparation, business math, and business administration is helpful

CERTIFICATION
- Cooks are required by law in most states to possess a health certificate and to be examined periodically. These examinations, usually given by the state board of health, make certain that you are free from communicable diseases and skin infections. The American Culinary Federation (ACF) offers certification at a variety of levels, such as executive chef and sous chef. Certification from ACF is recommended as a way to enhance your professional standing and advance your career.

RELATED JOBS/TITLES
- Chef
- Kitchen Helper
- Baker
- Executive Chef

EARNINGS
- Cooks: $12,150 to $17,090 to $26,050
- Restaurant cooks: $13,110 to $18,140 to $25,860

OUTLOOK
- According to the *Occupational Outlook Handbook,* jobs for institutional cooks are projected to grow more slowly than the average and for restaurant cooks about as fast as the average through 2010. Turnover rates are high, and the need to find replacement cooks will mean many job opportunities in all areas.

FOR MORE INFORMATION

For information on careers in baking and cooking, education, and certification, contact the following organizations:

American Culinary Federation, Inc.
10 San Bartola Drive
St. Augustine, FL 32086
800-624-9458
acf@acfchefs.net
http://www.acfchefs.org

Culinary Institute of America
1946 Campus Drive
Hyde Park, NY 12538-1499
845-452-9600
http://www.ciachef.edu

Educational Institute of the American Hotel and Lodging Association
800 North Magnolia Avenue, Suite 1800
Orlando, FL 32803
800-752-4567
info@ei-ahla.org
http://www.ei-ahla.org

National Restaurant Association Educational Foundation
175 West Jackson Boulevard, Suite 1500
Chicago, IL 60604-2702
800-765-2122
http://www.nraef.org

■ Construction Equipment Operator

A construction equipment operator drives machines that move materials and dirt as well as apply asphalt and concrete to roads and other areas. Duties vary depending on the job and machine being used, but may include paving, surfacing, loading, bulldozing, lifting, leveling, and operating forklifts, air compressors, and pumps. Other responsibilities include reading about and applying safety regulations, understanding diagrams and blueprints, and applying them to your work.

MAY BE GOOD FOR YOU NOW IF YOU

- Have operated heavy farm equipment in the past
- Enjoy the challenge and the adventure of operating heavy equipment in less-than-favorable conditions
- Like working outdoors

HELPFUL PERSONAL TRAITS

- Good eye-hand coordination
- Good health and physical condition
- Able to follow directions well
- Detail-oriented

VALUE TO YOUR CAREER DEVELOPMENT

- Can help meet values of achievement, power, and skill
- Satisfaction derived from meeting deadlines
- Satisfaction derived from handling the challenges presented by environmental conditions

VALUE TO EMPLOYER/SOCIETY

- Vital to the building and maintenance of the nation's highways, bridges, buildings, and other structures

POSSIBLE DOWNSIDES

- Noisy, dirty, dusty, greasy, and uncomfortable conditions
- Shaking and jolting may cause back problems
- May have to work long hours and be away from home for long periods

POPULATION GROUPS
- Part-Time/Temporary
- General

PREPARATION
- Job skills are usually learned on the job
- Mechanical and/or electronic background may be helpful
- Apprenticeship may offer a competitive edge

CERTIFICATION
- Certification is not usually associated with this occupation

RELATED JOBS/TITLES
- Operating Engineer
- Crane Operator
- Forklift Driver
- Bulldozer Driver
- Truck Driver

EARNINGS
- $20,810 to $33,250 to $56,760

OUTLOOK
- According to the *Occupational Outlook Handbook,* jobs for construction equipment operators are projected to increase more slowly than the average through 2010. This is due in part to the increased efficiency brought about by automation. The construction industry is very sensitive to changes in the overall economy, so the number of openings may fluctuate from year to year.

FOR MORE INFORMATION
For additional information, contact the following organizations:

Associated General Contractors of America
333 John Carlyle Street, Suite 200
Alexandria, VA 22314
703-548-3118
http://www.agc.org

■ Construction Laborer

A construction laborer performs tasks, usually outdoors, that require physical strength. Duties may include work on buildings, highway construction, excavation, hazardous waste removal, and demolition. Specific tasks can involve preparation of a construction site; digging; lifting, kneeling, and crawling; carrying materials; mixing and pouring concrete; loading and unloading materials; distributing building materials; climbing ladders; and walking on scaffolds. Hand and power tools used may include saws, torches, rakes, sledgehammers, pick axes, shovels, pavement breakers, jackhammers, pumps, and compressors.

MAY BE GOOD FOR YOU NOW IF YOU

■ Want to stay in good physical shape by doing heavy labor

■ Like to work outdoors

■ Prefer seasonal work

■ Grew up and worked on a farm

■ Are a college athlete who needs to earn money for school

HELPFUL PERSONAL TRAITS

■ Physically strong and in good health

■ Manual dexterity

■ Able to understand and follow directions well

■ Good at math

■ Alert

■ Dependable

VALUE TO YOUR CAREER DEVELOPMENT

■ Can help meet the values of achievement, health, skill, and loyalty

■ Gives a sense of pride and achievement after completing a construction project

VALUE TO EMPLOYER/SOCIETY

■ Often perform hard and dangerous work that many are unwilling and/or unable to do

■ Contributes to the beauty and attractiveness of communities

POSSIBLE DOWNSIDES
- Work can be dirty, dusty, noisy, and uncomfortable
- Lots of shaking and jolting
- Must sometimes work in poor weather
- May need to wear safety clothes, glasses, and shoes
- Long hours and possibly extended time away from family

POPULATION GROUPS
- Part-Time/Temporary
- Limited Disabled
- General

PREPARATION
- No formal education is required
- Skills can be learned informally on the job
- Apprenticeship is usually necessary for advancement
- May be asked to take drug test before entry

CERTIFICATION
- Certification is not usually associated with this occupation

RELATED JOBS/TITLES
- Materials Moving Worker
- Laborer
- Grounds Maintenance Worker
- Forest Worker
- Freight Mover

EARNINGS
- $15,020 to $23,200 to $45,510

OUTLOOK
- According to the *Occupational Outlook Handbook,* jobs for construction laborers are projected to grow about as fast as the average through 2010. This is a large field, and turnover is high. For this reason, every year there will be jobs available, mainly in connection with large projects, because employers need to replace those workers who have changed jobs or left the labor

force. In addition, the level of construction activity is always affected by local economic conditions.

FOR MORE INFORMATION

For information about contractor careers, contact:

Associated General Contractors of America
333 John Carlyle Street, Suite 200
Alexandria, VA 22314
703-548-3118
info@agc.org
http://www.agc.org

For information on the role of union membership in construction jobs, check out this union's Web site:

Laborers' International Union of North America
905 16th Street, NW
Washington, DC 20006
202-737-8320
http://www.liuna.org

■ Corrections Officer

A corrections officer assists administrators in jails, reformatories, and prisons by performing tasks that ensure the safety and security of individuals who have been arrested (includes those who are awaiting trial, have been convicted of a crime, and have been sentenced to serve time). Duties usually include accounting for inmate activities, maintaining order, giving verbal instructions, being sure that inmates comply with rules and regulations, escorting prisoners to and from various destinations, and submitting reports.

MAY BE GOOD FOR YOU NOW IF YOU

- Desire experience in a correctional environment in preparation for a career in law enforcement or criminal justice

- Desire to participate in the effort to make positive changes in correctional facilities

HELPFUL PERSONAL TRAITS

- Good communication skills

- Trustworthy

- Able to make good judgments

- Conscientious

- Able to persuade and influence others

- Fair and respectful toward others

VALUE TO YOUR CAREER DEVELOPMENT

- Can help to meet the values of justice, safety, and helping others

- Satisfaction derived from knowing you perform a key role in the ongoing effort to maintain law and order

VALUE TO EMPLOYER/SOCIETY

- Helps to protect society from those who may inflict harm on others and/or their property

POSSIBLE DOWNSIDES

- May not often receive positive recognition for efforts

- Possible danger to your physical safety and health

POPULATION GROUPS
■ General

PREPARATION
■ Must have high school diploma or GED
■ Must be a U.S. citizen, be physically fit, and have committed no felonies
■ Usually must pass a civil service exam and take a drug test
■ On-the-job training and instructional program usually provided by the employer

CERTIFICATION
■ Short-term certificate programs may be available in some community colleges. A few states require passing a written examination. Corrections officers who work for the federal government and most state governments are covered by civil service systems or merit boards and may be required to pass a competitive exam for employment.

RELATED JOBS/TITLES
■ Security Guard
■ Police Officer
■ Detention Officer
■ Parole Officer

EARNINGS
■ $20,010 to $31,170 to $49,310

OUTLOOK
■ According to the *Occupational Outlook Handbook,* jobs for corrections officers are projected to increase faster than the average through 2010. Many job openings will occur from a characteristically high turnover rate. Traditionally, correction agencies have difficulty attracting qualified employees due to job location and salary considerations. Employment in this field is not usually affected by poor economic conditions or changes in government spending. Corrections officers are rarely laid off, even when budgets need to be trimmed.

FOR MORE INFORMATION

For information on training, conferences, and membership, contact:

American Correctional Association
4380 Forbes Boulevard
Lanham, MD 20706
301-918-1800
http://www.corrections.comaca

American Probation and Parole Association
PO Box 11910
2760 Research Park Drive
Lexington, KY 40511-8410
859-244-8203
appa@csg.org
http://www.appa-net.org

For information on entrance requirements, training, and career opportunities for corrections officers at the federal level, contact:

Federal Bureau of Prisons
320 First Street, NW
Washington, DC 20534
202-307-3198
http://www.bop.gov

This Web site bills itself as the "Largest Online Resource for News and Information in Corrections."

The Corrections Connection
http://www.corrections.com

■ Cosmetologist

Cosmetologists perform personal grooming tasks for both men and women. They cut and style hair, beards, and sideburns; straighten hair or apply permanent wave; shampoo and condition hair; and give grooming advice. Other tasks may include fitting hairpieces, hair coloring, and scalp treatment. Some may provide skin care, nail treatment, make-up application analysis, and eyebrow shaping.

MAY BE GOOD FOR YOU NOW IF YOU
- Desire to be self-employed
- Can already cut hair well, have been doing it for friends, and enjoy it
- Desire to work part-time
- Enjoy making others look good

HELPFUL PERSONAL TRAITS
- Friendly and outgoing
- Like to be neat, clean, and well groomed
- Physical stamina
- Creative and flexible

VALUE TO YOUR CAREER DEVELOPMENT
- Can help meet the values of personal appearance, esthetics, achievement, and recognition
- Can provide personal satisfaction of knowing that your service often lifts the spirits of your clients

VALUE TO EMPLOYER/SOCIETY
- Contributes to the emotional well-being and self-esteem of customers
- Contributes to making others look and feel better

POSSIBLE DOWNSIDES
- Required weekend and evening work
- Long hours
- Must stand for long periods

POPULATION GROUPS
- Part-Time/Temporary
- Ex-Offender
- General

PREPARATION
- All states require licensure
- Must graduate from a state-licensed school
- Must be at least 16 years old
- Continuing education will be necessary to stay abreast of changing trends

CERTIFICATION
- At the completion of the proper number of credit hours, you must pass a formal written examination to become licensed. Some states also require a practical (hands-on) test and oral exams. State board examinations are given at regular intervals.

  Many states require licensed cosmetologists to take a specified number of credit hours, called continuing-education units or CEUs. Licenses must be renewed in all states, generally every year or every two years.

  In the majority of states, the minimum age for an individual to obtain a cosmetology license is 16. Because standards and requirements vary from state to state, students are urged to contact the licensing board of the state in which they plan to be employed.

RELATED JOBS/TITLES
- Barber
- Hair Stylist
- Hairdresser
- Make-Up Artist
- Manicurist
- Skin Care Specialist
- Nail Technician

EARNINGS
- Cosmetologists: $12,280 to $17,660 to $33,220
- Barbers: $12,030 to $17,740 to $33,040

OUTLOOK

■ According to the *Occupational Outlook Handbook,* jobs for cosmetologists are expected to grow about as fast as the average through 2010. Turnover in this career is fairly high, as cosmetologists move into management positions, change careers, or leave the field for other reasons. Competition for jobs at higher-paying, prestigious salons is strong.

FOR MORE INFORMATION

Contact the following organizations for more information on cosmetology careers:

American Association of Cosmetology Schools
15825 North 71st Street, Suite 100
Scottsdale, AZ 85254-1521
800-831-1086
http://www.beautyschools.org

Beauty and Barber Supply Institute, Inc.
15825 North 71st Street, Suite 100
Scottsdale, AZ 85254
800-468-2274
http://www.bbsi.org

National Accrediting Commission of Cosmetology Arts and Sciences
4401 Ford Avenue, Suite 1300
Arlington, VA 22302-1432
703-600-7600
http://www.naccas.org

National Cosmetology Association
401 North Michigan Avenue
Chicago, IL 60611
312-527-6765
http://www.salonprofessionals.org

For fun facts on hairstyling, visit the following Web site:

Hair International
http://www.hairinternational.com

■ Counter Clerk

Counter clerks wait on customers at retail establishments. The most common workplaces are storage businesses; cleaners; rental stores, including video stores; recreational establishments; alteration shops; and service departments. Duties vary depending on the products or services but could include taking orders, determining and/or receiving fees, quoting rates, providing information or instructions, locating and presenting merchandise to customers, and verifying rental contract fulfillment. Clerks sometimes prepare billing statements to be sent to customers, keep records of receipts and sales throughout the day, and balance the money in their registers when their work shift ends.

MAY BE GOOD FOR YOU NOW IF YOU

- Want to volunteer
- Need to make extra money for school
- Have some experience and enjoy working with the public
- Want to work part-time, evenings, or weekends
- Plan to eventually have a career in sales, customer service, or public relations

HELPFUL PERSONAL TRAITS

- Pleasant and friendly
- Tactful and courteous
- Good verbal skills
- Quick to learn
- Honest
- Patient

VALUE TO YOUR CAREER DEVELOPMENT

- May help meet the values of knowledge, serving others, and recognition
- Satisfaction derived from positive customer feedback about the service you rendered
- Satisfaction derived from calming angry customers and making them happy

VALUE TO EMPLOYER/SOCIETY
- Provides a valuable public relations function
- As a front-line employee, you often influence customers' decisions to return for repeat business

POSSIBLE DOWNSIDES
- Can be stressful during busy hours and when customers become angry
- Must stand for extended periods
- Possible exposure to crime when handling money in a public place

POPULATION GROUPS
- Part-Time/Temporary
- Senior Citizen
- Volunteer
- General

PREPARATION
- Requires little or no experience
- Usually on-the-job training is provided
- A high school diploma is preferred, although not required
- Previous work with the public is helpful

CERTIFICATION
- Certification is not usually associated with this occupation

RELATED JOBS/TITLES
- Rental Clerk
- Information Clerk
- Parts Clerk
- Retail Salesperson
- Postal Service Clerk
- Teller
- Cashier

EARNINGS
- $12,070 to $16,370 to $28,610

OUTLOOK
- According to the *Occupational Outlook Handbook,* jobs for counter clerks are projected to increase about as fast as the average through 2010. Major employers should be those that provide rental products and services, such as car rental firms, video rental stores, and other equipment rental businesses. Because of the high turnover in this field, many job openings will come from the need to replace workers. Opportunities for temporary or part-time work should be good. Jobs for clerks are plentiful in large metropolitan areas.

FOR MORE INFORMATION
For information about educational programs in the retail industry, contact:

National Retail Federation
325 7th Street, NW, Suite 1100
Washington, DC 20004
800-NRF-4692
http://www.nrf.com

■ Customer Service Representative

Customer service representatives respond to customer inquiries about a company's, agency's, or institution's products and services. They spend a significant amount of their time resolving customer complaints or concerns. In addition, duties usually include providing information, directions, and instructions; providing assistance of all kinds; making recommendations; and maintaining records.

MAY BE GOOD FOR YOU NOW IF YOU

■ Want to work part-time or flexible hours

■ Like to solve problems

■ Want to gain experience working with people who may be unhappy with a service

■ Plan to become a customer service manager

HELPFUL PERSONAL TRAITS

■ Courteous and tactful

■ Good telephone etiquette

■ Patient

■ Able to make sound judgments

■ Good listener

■ Friendly

■ Excellent communication skills

■ Good people skills

VALUE TO YOUR CAREER DEVELOPMENT

■ Can help meet the values of justice, achievement, kindness, and serving others

■ Can help you develop patience

■ Satisfaction derived from helping people resolve issues

VALUE TO EMPLOYER/SOCIETY

■ Could help minimize expenses by helping to reduce returns and repairs

■ Can be crucial to a company's reputation, sales, and overall success

POSSIBLE DOWNSIDES
- May have to work evenings or weekends
- May experience high stress as a result of working with angry customers

POPULATION GROUPS
- Part-Time/Temporary
- Single Parent
- Senior Citizen
- General

PREPARATION
- No formal training required
- Employer provides on-the-job training
- Good people skills as well as computer and clerical proficiency are helpful

CERTIFICATION
- The International Customer Service Association offers a voluntary certification as a Certified Customer Service Professional (CCSP)

RELATED JOBS/TITLES
- Customer Service Specialist
- Sales Representative
- Customer Complaint Clerk
- Adjustment Clerk
- Processing Clerk

EARNINGS
- $16,080 to $24,600 to $40,690

OUTLOOK
- According to the *Occupational Outlook Handbook,* jobs for customer service representatives are projected to increase faster than the average through 2010. There is high turnover of workers in this field. In addition, the Internet and e-commerce should increase the need for customer service representatives to help

customers navigate Web sites, answer questions over the phone, and respond to emails.

FOR MORE INFORMATION

For information on customer service and other support positions, contact:

Association of Support Professionals
66 Mt. Auburn Street
Watertown, MA 02472
617-924-3944, ext. 11
http://www.asponline.com

For information on jobs, training, workshops, and salaries, contact:

Customer Care Institute
17 Dean Overlook, NW
Atlanta, GA 30318
404-352-9291
info@customercare.com
http://www.customercare.com

For information about the customer service industry, contact:

Help Desk Institute
6385 Corporate Drive, Suite 301
Colorado Springs, CO 80919
800-248-5667
http://www.helpdeskinst.com

For more information on international customer service careers and certification, contact:

International Customer Service Association
401 North Michigan Avenue
Chicago, IL 60611
800-360-4272
http://www.icsa.com

■ Fast Food Worker

A fast food worker performs both customer-service and food-preparation tasks in restaurants that provide customers with meals in a very short time period. Duties usually include taking orders, cooking and preparing food, bagging and/or serving food, operating a cash register, taking and receiving payment and making change, and operating fountain equipment or drink machines. Some may make coffee and perform cleaning or related housekeeping tasks.

MAY BE GOOD FOR YOU NOW IF YOU

- Are a high school or college student who needs a part-time job
- Are a senior citizen and need to supplement your current income or improve your lifestyle
- Want to work part-time, evenings, and weekends

HELPFUL PERSONAL TRAITS

- Pleasant and friendly
- Polite and patient
- Good memory
- Able to react quickly
- Good people skills
- Good speaking and listening skills
- Work well under pressure

VALUE TO YOUR CAREER DEVELOPMENT

- Can help meet the values of serving others, achievement, and knowledge
- Can learn work skills necessary for any job
- Can help you learn patience and how to maintain composure under pressure

VALUE TO EMPLOYER/SOCIETY

- Provides quick, convenient meals in a fast-paced society
- Older workers may model a level of wisdom and maturity that can influence younger workers which, in turn, can result in higher work quality and worker retention
- Provides many people with their first paying job

POSSIBLE DOWNSIDES
- Low wages
- Must be on your feet most of the time
- Danger of burns, cuts, slips, and falls
- Can cause high stress during rush hours
- May not get positive recognition you desire

POPULATION GROUPS
- Part-Time/Temporary
- Limited Disabled
- Immigrant/Refugee
- Senior Citizen
- General

PREPARATION
- No formal education is required for this occupation
- On-the-job training is normally provided by the employer

CERTIFICATION
- Certification is not usually associated with this occupation

RELATED JOBS/TITLES
- Fast Food Assistant
- Counter Attendant
- Food Service Preparation Worker
- Host/Hostess
- Server
- Cashier

EARNINGS
- $10,712 to $15,350 to $22,152

OUTLOOK
- According to the *Occupational Outlook Handbook,* jobs for fast food workers are projected to grow as fast as the average through 2010. Turnover is high in these jobs for a number of reasons, including the low pay, the long hours, and the large number of students and others who do this work on a temporary basis

before moving on to other occupations. Entry-level jobs are not difficult to find. Submitting an application and keeping in touch with managers for openings can lead to the beginning of a successful career in the fast food industry.

FOR MORE INFORMATION

Visit this association's Web site for information on the restaurant industry (including fast-food establishments), food safety, and government regulations.

National Restaurant Association
1200 17th Street, NW
Washington, DC 20036
202-331-5900
http://www.restaurant.org

This trade association offers information on food service employee requirements and training.

National Restaurant Association Educational Foundation
175 West Jackson Boulevard, Suite 1500
Chicago, IL 60604-2702
800-765-2122
http://www.edfound.org

■ Food Server

A food server serves food and beverages to customers and performs a variety of related tasks in eating places of all types and sizes. Duties vary depending on the size, type, and location of the establishment but normally include preparing and cleaning tables, greeting and seating customers, taking orders, serving food, describing menu items and answering questions, refilling beverage containers, and taking payment from and returning change to customers. A server's job is to make the customer's experience as comfortable and enjoyable as possible.

MAY BE GOOD FOR YOU NOW IF YOU

■ Want to work part-time, evenings, and weekends

■ Are especially good with people

■ Need supplemental income to assist with school or home expenses

■ Want to gain experience as you prepare for a career in hospitality

HELPFUL PERSONAL TRAITS

■ Strong communication skills

■ Desire to please others

■ Able to accept public scrutiny and criticism

■ Good at taking orders and remembering

■ Good eye-hand coordination

■ Thoughtful and tactful

■ Friendly

■ Quick and sure-footed

VALUE TO YOUR CAREER DEVELOPMENT

■ May help meet the values of serving others and recognition

■ Can provide supplemental income

■ Gain appreciation and recognition from others

VALUE TO EMPLOYER/SOCIETY

■ Helps many Americans to experience a respite from their day-to-day routine

■ May contribute to the social fulfillment and emotional well-being of customers

▪ Contributes to an industry that is significant to the country's economic health and to the American way of life

POSSIBLE DOWNSIDES
▪ May have to work holidays, weekends, and late evenings
▪ Must be on your feet and moving quickly most of the time
▪ Danger of slips, falls, and burns
▪ Must carry and balance heavy food trays

POPULATION GROUPS
▪ Part-Time/Temporary
▪ Single Parent
▪ Degree Complement

PREPARATION
▪ No formal training is required
▪ Skills are learned on the job

CERTIFICATION
▪ Certification is not usually associated with this occupation Food service workers almost always are required to obtain health certificates from the state Department of Public Health to verify they are free from communicable diseases, as shown by physical examination and blood tests. This is required for the protection of the general public.

RELATED JOBS/TITLES
▪ Host/Hostess
▪ Waiter/Waitress
▪ Dining Room Attendant
▪ Flight Attendant
▪ Busperson
▪ Caterer

EARNINGS
▪ $4,430 to $13,580 to $21,110+ (plus tips)

OUTLOOK
▪ According to the *Occupational Outlook Handbook,* jobs for servers are projected to grow about as fast as the average through

2010. Turnover is high in these jobs because of the low pay, the long hours, and the large number of students and others who do this work on a temporary basis before moving on to other occupations. Seasonal job opportunities are available in summer or winter resort areas. Jobs for beginning workers are more plentiful in lower-priced restaurants.

FOR MORE INFORMATION

For information on the hospitality industry and career opportunities, contact:

American Hotel and Lodging Association
1201 New York Avenue, NW, Suite 600
Washington, DC 20005-3931
202-289-3100
informationcenter@ahla.com
http://www.ahma.com

American Hotel and Lodging Foundation
1201 New York Avenue, NW, Suite 600
Washington, DC 20005-3931
202-289-3180
ahlf@ahlf.org
http://www.ahlf.org

For information on job opportunities and accredited education programs, contact:

International Council on Hotel, Restaurant, and Institutional Education
2613 North Parham Road, 2nd Floor
Richmond, VA 23294
804-346-4800
info@chrie.org
http://chrie.org

For information on education, scholarships, and careers, contact:

National Restaurant Association Educational Foundation
175 West Jackson Boulevard, Suite 1500
Chicago, IL 60604-2702
800-765-2122
info@foodtrain.org
http://www.nraef.org

■ Groundskeeper

A groundskeeper maintains the grounds around homes, office buildings, parks, athletic fields, golf courses, and college campuses, along highways, and at various other sites. Duties vary depending on the location but usually include some or all of the following: maintaining walkways, drives, and parking lots; mowing; trimming and pruning; watering; fertilizing; maintaining soil; planting trees, shrubs, and lawns; raking and mulching leaves; sweeping; cleaning and picking up debris; and shoveling snow. Other tasks include maintenance of pools, fountains, fences, plants, benches, and equipment.

MAY BE GOOD FOR YOU NOW IF YOU
■ Like to be outdoors

■ Want part-time and/or seasonal work

■ Have a "green thumb"

■ Have good vision

■ Plan to eventually become a landscape architect or start your own landscaping business

HELPFUL PERSONAL TRAITS
■ Have a deep appreciation for nature

■ Enjoy gardening

■ Physical stamina

■ Manual dexterity

■ Tend to be neat

■ Creative

■ Get along well with people

VALUE TO YOUR CAREER DEVELOPMENT
■ Can help meet the values of esthetics, achievement, personal appearance, and independence

■ Satisfaction derived from working outdoors

■ Satisfaction derived from creating and maintaining an environment that lifts people's spirits

VALUE TO EMPLOYER/SOCIETY
■ Contributes to the beauty and value of property

- Quality of grounds can attract or discourage patronage or visitations, which can significantly impact business success
- An attractively maintained environment can contribute to the emotional well-being of others

POSSIBLE DOWNSIDES
- Can be physically tiring and involve a lot of lifting, climbing, bending, and shoveling
- Sometimes pressure to meet deadlines
- May be exposed to dangers of working with machinery and pesticides
- Low wages

POPULATION GROUPS
- Part-Time/Temporary
- Ex-Offender
- Limited Disabled
- General

PREPARATION
- No formal education is usually required
- Job skills are learned on the job
- May need certification to regularly apply pesticides

CERTIFICATION
- The Associated Landscape Contractors of America offers Certified Landscape Professional (Exterior and Interior), Certified Landscape Technician (Exterior), and Certified Landscape Technician (Interior) designations.

   The Professional Grounds Management Society offers Certified Grounds Manager (CGM) certification and the Certified Grounds Keeper (CGK) certification.

   Some states require grounds workers to pass a certification examination on the proper application of pesticides, fungicides, and other harsh chemicals.

RELATED JOBS/TITLES
- Groundskeeping Worker
- Landscape Gardener

- Greenskeeper
- Grounds Maintenance Worker
- Agricultural Worker
- Landscape Architect

EARNINGS
- $13,600 to $18,300 to $29,420

OUTLOOK
- According to the *Occupational Outlook Handbook,* jobs for groundskeepers are projected to be in abundance and to grow faster than the average through 2010. Growth is expected in the construction of commercial and industrial buildings, homes, highways, and recreational facilities. A high turnover rate in groundskeeping occupations creates many opportunities for employment.

FOR MORE INFORMATION
For job listings and information on certification and career placement, contact:

American Society for Horticultural Sciences
113 South West Street, Suite 200
Alexandria, VA 22314-2851
703-836-4606
ashscph@ashs.org
http://www.ashs.org

For information on certification, contact:

Associated Landscape Contractors of America
150 Elden Street, Suite 270
Herndon, VA 20170
800-395-2522
http://www.alca.org

For information on student membership and certification, contact:

Professional Grounds Management Society
720 Light Street
Baltimore, MD 21230
800-609-7467
pgms@assnhqtrs.com
http://www.pgms.org

■ Hand Packer/Packager

A hand packer/packager is a materials moving worker who packs, packages, and/or wraps materials. Other tasks may include checking for defects, labeling, stamping, stacking, bagging, moving packages, carrying bags to customer's vehicles, filling orders, maintaining records, and sorting and cleaning containers.

MAY BE GOOD FOR YOU NOW IF YOU
- Have limited skills
- Need to develop a work record
- Don't mind doing physical work
- Want to work part-time

HELPFUL PERSONAL TRAITS
- Good eye-hand coordination
- Aptitude for basic math and reading
- Good health
- Responsible
- Neat
- Good at understanding and following instructions

VALUE TO YOUR CAREER DEVELOPMENT
- Can help meet the values of achievement and helping others
- Satisfaction derived from completing a task, getting an order out, and packing something of value so that it will not be damaged en route

VALUE TO EMPLOYER/SOCIETY
- Contributes to the important process of getting goods to and from their destinations efficiently and without damage

POSSIBLE DOWNSIDES
- May be repetitive and strenuous
- Involves lifting, carrying, and bending
- Must stand for long periods
- Low pay

POPULATION GROUPS
- Part-Time/Temporary
- Ex-Offender
- Limited Disabled
- General

PREPARATION
- Usually requires no work experience or specific training
- Tasks can be learned on the job in a short period of time

CERTIFICATION
- Certification is not usually associated with this job

RELATED JOBS/TITLES
- Packer
- Assembler
- Bagger
- Material Mover
- Stock Clerk

EARNINGS
- $12,030 to $15,660 to $24,540

OUTLOOK
- According to the *Occupational Outlook Handbook,* jobs for hand packers/packagers, included in the category of material moving occupations, are projected to grow about as fast as the average through 2010. Increased automation and more efficient production methods will lessen the demand for these workers, but turnover is high, so job openings should be plentiful.

FOR MORE INFORMATION
For information about job opportunities and training programs, contact state employment service offices, building or construction contractors, manufacturers, and wholesale and retail establishments.

■ Highway Maintenance Worker

Highway maintenance workers perform maintenance tasks on highways, city and rural roads, and airport runways. Duties may include patching and fixing broken pavement, repairing and erecting guard rails, placing highway markers, fixing snow fences, clearing brush, and planting trees. Some highway maintenance workers drive trucks to transport workers and equipment, forklifts, tractors with mowers, snow plows, sewer cleaners, and other equipment. Tools of the trade include posthole diggers, shovels, axes, saws, hammers, and various power tools.

MAY BE GOOD FOR YOU NOW IF YOU
■ Enjoy working outdoors
■ Want to stay in shape during the off-season of a sport you participate in
■ Want seasonal work

HELPFUL PERSONAL TRAITS
■ Like to do physical work
■ Careful
■ Physical stamina and good health
■ Good working with hands

VALUE TO YOUR CAREER DEVELOPMENT
■ Could help meet esthetic value by being outdoors and being exposed to nature
■ Provides a service that could prevent vehicle accidents and injury and give support to the values of health and safety

VALUE TO EMPLOYER/SOCIETY
■ Maintains safe conditions on and around highways, which helps prevent numerous injuries and even deaths that could be caused by poor road conditions
■ Indirectly, a state's reputation for having good, safe roads may result in more travelers from other states who may increase revenues for businesses as well as the state

POSSIBLE DOWNSIDES
■ May have to work in bad weather and around insects
■ Requires heavy physical work

- May have to work around dangerous machines, equipment, and hazardous materials and in traffic

POPULATION GROUPS
- Part-Time/Temporary
- Ex-Offender
- Limited Disabled
- General

PREPARATION
- Short-term training is usually provided on the job
- A good driving record and a valid license to drive is necessary for those who drive trucks and operate other vehicles

CERTIFICATION
- Certification is not usually associated with this occupation

RELATED JOBS/TITLES
- Helper
- Laborer
- Rail Track Maintenance Worker
- Paving and Surfacing Equipment Operator
- Pile Driver Operator

EARNINGS
- $16,370 to $26,660 to $40,740

OUTLOOK
- According to the *Occupational Outlook Handbook,* jobs for highway maintenance workers are projected to increase more slowly than average through 2010. This is a large field, and turnover is high among these workers. For these reasons, every year there will be jobs available, mainly in connection with large projects, because employers need to replace those workers who have changed jobs or left the labor force.

FOR MORE INFORMATION
For information about contractor careers, contact:

Associated General Contractors of America
333 John Carlyle Street, Suite 200
Alexandria, VA 22314
703-548-3118
info@agc.org
http://www.agc.org

For information on the role of union membership in construction jobs, check this union's Web site:

Laborers' International Union of North America
905 16th Street, NW
Washington, DC 20006
202-737-8320
http://www.liuna.org

■ Home Care Aide

Home care aides perform tasks and errands to help people who are usually elderly, disabled, ill, or homebound. Their assistance allows patients and clients to live in their homes. Aides work in a variety of settings, from homes where a parent is unable to care for small children or in the residences of recently discharged hospital patients. Duties may involve cleaning, planning meals, cooking, doing laundry, helping a patient bathe and dress, helping a patient stand and walk, assisting a patient with medications, shopping, and listening and providing companionship.

MAY BE GOOD FOR YOU NOW IF YOU
■ Want to work part-time

■ Like to help those who cannot help themselves

■ Like to work hard and don't mind working in possibly unpleasant situations

HELPFUL PERSONAL TRAITS
■ Gentle

■ Compassionate

■ Patient, particularly with the elderly and those with disabilities

■ Sensitive to the needs and pains of others

■ Tactful and discreet

■ Work well in stressful situations

■ Emotionally strong

VALUE TO YOUR CAREER DEVELOPMENT
■ Can help meet values of helping and serving others, love, and recognition

■ Satisfaction derived from appreciation expressed by those who receive your care

VALUE TO EMPLOYER/SOCIETY
■ Direct and personal help given to those who need it is a service greatly appreciated by most

■ Helps to meet a critical need in our country as the population becomes increasingly older and in need of such services

■ Helps to meet the need for outpatient care as hospitals and insurance companies shorten hospital stays and cut inpatient services

POSSIBLE DOWNSIDES

■ Sometimes unpleasant—patients can be disoriented or uncooperative

■ May be susceptible to falls and injuries from lifting and carrying

■ May have to travel

■ Low wages and little chance for advancement

POPULATION GROUPS

■ Part-Time/Temporary

■ Single Parent

■ Volunteer

■ General

PREPARATION

■ Usually no formal academic requirements are needed for entry

■ Some states require a physical and/or background check

CERTIFICATION

■ Certification is not usually associated with this occupation

RELATED JOBS/TITLES

■ Homemaker

■ Nursing Aide

■ Home Health Care Aide

■ Personal Attendant

■ Caregiver

EARNINGS

■ $11,940 to $15,600 to $21,080

OUTLOOK

■ According to the *Occupational Outlook Handbook,* jobs for home care aides are projected to grow much faster than average through 2010. Because of the physical and emotional demands of the job, there is high turnover and, therefore, there are frequent job openings for home care aides.

FOR MORE INFORMATION
For information about a career as a home care aide and schools offering training, contact:

National Association of Health Career Schools
750 First Street, NE, Suite 940
Washington, DC 20002
202-842-1592
nahcs@aol.com
http://www.nahcs.org

For details on home care careers, contact this organization or check its Web site:

National Association for Home Care
228 Seventh Street, SE
Washington, DC 20003
202-547-7424
http://www.nahc.org

■ Home Health Care Aide

A home health care aide enables the elderly, convalescent, or people with disabilities to live in their own homes rather than health care facilities. While a number of the duties performed are similar to what a home care aide does, the primary difference is that a home health care aide works under the supervision of nursing or medical staff and conducts a number of health-related activities. Responsibilities include checking pulse and respiration; helping with exercises and movement of patients; bathing, dressing, and grooming patients; administering oral medications; giving massages; and assisting with medical equipment.

MAY BE GOOD FOR YOU NOW IF YOU

- Are a retiree from this or a similar occupation and want to return as a volunteer
- Desire to help those who cannot help themselves
- Plan to become a nurse or related health professional

HELPFUL PERSONAL TRAITS

- Compassionate
- Gentle
- Honest
- Able to work independently
- Have good health and vision
- Dependable
- Patient
- Good communication skills
- Discreet

VALUE TO YOUR CAREER DEVELOPMENT

- May help to meet values of helping others, health, love, and recognition
- Satisfaction derived from helping others and being appreciated for doing so

VALUE TO EMPLOYER/SOCIETY

- Meets a critical health care need in the United States today

■ Enables many people who are ill, elderly, or disabled to remain in their familiar home settings

POSSIBLE DOWNSIDES

■ Must stand for extended periods and do a lot of walking

■ Some tasks may be unpleasant

■ May be at risk for back strain and muscle injuries caused by lifting and carrying

■ Low pay

■ May have to drive considerable distances to and from home sites

■ Possible risk of contracting infections and diseases if safety measures are not practiced

POPULATION GROUPS

■ Part-Time/Temporary

■ Single Parent

■ Volunteer

■ General

PREPARATION

■ No prior experience or formal education is required for entry

CERTIFICATION

■ Certification is not usually associated with this occupation. The National Association for Home Care offers voluntary certification for home care and hospice executives, which demonstrates a defined level of education, knowledge, and experience.

RELATED JOBS/TITLES

■ Caregiver

■ Home Care Aide

■ Nursing Aide

■ Personal Attendant

■ Psychiatric Aide

EARNINGS

■ $12,770 to $17,120 to $24,810

OUTLOOK

■ According to the *Occupational Outlook Handbook,* jobs for home health care aides are projected to grow faster than the average through 2010. Because of the physical and emotional demands of the job and the low pay, there is high turnover in this occupation.

FOR MORE INFORMATION

For information about a career as a home health care aide and schools offering training, contact:

National Association of Health Career Schools
750 First Street, NE, Suite 940
Washington, DC 20002
202-842-1592
nahcs@aol.com
http://www.nahcs.org

For details on certification and statistics on home health care careers, contact or check the following Web site:

National Association for Home Care
228 Seventh Street, SE
Washington, DC 20003
202-547-7424
http://www.nahc.org

■ Hotel/Motel Clerk

Hotel and motel clerks greet and assist guests and visitors and provide them with information about services and amenities. Although specific duties vary, tasks may include giving advice and instructions concerning room location, services, and dining facilities and providing directions to entertainment sites and nearby points of interest. Other duties include checking customers in and out; responding to inquiries; resolving minor concerns and conflicts; arranging for tours; booking reservations at restaurants, theaters, and other special events; and securing the possessions of guests. Hotel and motel clerks also may provide complementary items; operate computers; answer phone calls; keep records; and perform other clerical tasks.

MAY BE GOOD FOR YOU NOW IF YOU
■ Want to pursue a career in hospitality

■ Like to meet all types of people

■ Want to work part-time or flexible hours

HELPFUL PERSONAL TRAITS
■ Cheerful and friendly

■ Good organizational and memory skills

■ Team player

■ Professional demeanor

■ Excellent communication skills

■ Willingness to go the "extra mile"

VALUE TO YOUR CAREER DEVELOPMENT
■ Can help meet the values of hospitality, helping others, and pleasure

■ Satisfaction derived from helping others to acquire rest, relaxation, and pleasure.

■ Satisfaction derived from being able to offer a place to stay for weary travelers

VALUE TO EMPLOYER/SOCIETY
■ Some establishments are entry ports for international visitors and can make a positive first impression

■ Contributes to the pleasure and emotional well-being of millions every year who need respite from the sometimes stressful pace of American life

■ Provides important services for many business travelers who attend conferences and meetings held in hotels

POSSIBLE DOWNSIDES

■ Occasionally have to deal with angry guests

■ May be on your feet for long periods

■ Long periods of time on a computer may cause eye strain

■ Low wages

POPULATION GROUPS

■ Part-Time/Temporary

■ General

PREPARATION

■ A high school diploma or equivalent is usually the minimum requirement

■ For advancement, home study courses in lodging management may be helpful; many in this industry are promoted from within

CERTIFICATION

■ Certification is not a requirement for this occupation, although it is considered by many employers as a measure of industry knowledge and experience. Programs like those offered by the Educational Institute of the American Hotel and Lodging Association are designed to help improve job performance and advancement potential and keep you up to date on industry changes. The Registry program is specifically designed for desk clerks and other entry-level positions.

Some community and technical colleges offer certification programs in hospitality-related occupations.

RELATED JOBS/TITLES

■ Hotel Receptionist

■ Desk Clerk

■ Information Clerk

■ Clerk

■ Reservation Clerk

- Teller
- Receptionist
- Customer Service Representative
- Travel Clerk
- Rental Clerk
- Counter Clerk

EARNINGS
- $12,370 to $16,380 to $22,570

OUTLOOK
- According to the *Occupational Outlook Handbook,* employment of hotel desk clerks is expected to grow faster than the average through 2010. While hotel bookings are down since the terrorist events of September 11, 2001, most industry experts believe the slowdown is temporary. The economic recession also has had an effect on both business and pleasure travel, although some recovery is expected within the next several years. These trends may affect employment of desk clerks, but people still need to travel for business and pleasure, so plenty of jobs should be available, particularly at hotels in busy urban areas, where there tend to be higher turnover rates. Larger hotels are known to pay higher wages, promote faster, and be more open to sending employees to further education classes and seminars.

FOR MORE INFORMATION
For career opportunities, certification, or educational information, contact:

American Hotel and Lodging Association
1201 New York Avenue, NW, Suite 600
Washington, DC 20005-3931
202-289-3100
http://www.ahla.com

For information on scholarships, contact:

American Hotel and Lodging Foundation
1201 New York Avenue, NW, Suite 600
Washington, DC 20005-3931
202-289-3180
http://www.ahlf.org

For a listing of schools with programs in hotel management, contact:

**International Council on Hotel, Restaurant and
Institutional Education**
2613 North Parham Road, 2nd Floor
Richmond, VA 23294
804-346-4800
http://chrie.org

*For career information and development and training programs,
contact:*

**Educational Institute of the American Hotel and
Lodging Association**
800 North Magnolia Avenue, Suite 1800
Orlando, FL 32803
800-752-4567
http://www.ei-ahla.org

■ Janitor

The duties of a janitor vary greatly and depend on the needs of a particular building. However, most janitors usually perform general maintenance and cleaning tasks in buildings of all types, including offices, hospitals, schools, apartments, hotels, and stores. Tasks can include cleaning restrooms, classrooms, offices, stairways, doorways, halls, entryways, walls, and floors. Other common tasks are emptying trash, mowing lawns, cleaning windows, dusting, moving furniture, lifting and setting up equipment, conducting minor repairs, and replenishing bathroom supplies.

MAY BE GOOD FOR YOU NOW IF YOU
- Need to work part-time or temporarily
- Need to develop a work history
- Enjoy cleaning
- Want to volunteer

HELPFUL PERSONAL TRAITS
- Good at following directions
- Trustworthy and responsible
- Eager and quick to learn
- Can work independently and without much supervision

VALUE TO YOUR CAREER DEVELOPMENT
- May help realize the values of safety, esthetics, physical appearance, health, and helping others
- Can contribute to a more positive sense of emotional well-being

VALUE TO EMPLOYER/SOCIETY
- A well-maintained facility and surrounding grounds can attract/retain employees, customers, businesses, students, etc.
- Minimizes the possibility of injuries due to lack of repair or poor maintenance

POSSIBLE DOWNSIDES
- Exposure to unpleasant or unhealthy situations
- May have to do heavy lifting

■ May be at risk for bruises, cuts, or chemical burns from working with tools or cleaning chemicals, as well as being at risk for back injuries from lifting and moving heavy objects

POPULATION GROUPS
■ Part-Time/Temporary
■ Limited Disabled
■ Single Parent
■ Ex-Offender
■ General

PREPARATION
■ No formal education is required for most janitorial jobs
■ Skills are normally learned on the job
■ Manual skills and a good grasp of arithmetic are helpful

CERTIFICATION
■ Although not a requirement for finding a job, some janitors become certified by the International Executive Housekeepers Association (IEHA). IEHA offers two levels of certification: the Certified Executive Housekeeper and the Registered Executive Housekeeper.

RELATED JOBS/TITLES
■ Building Custodian
■ Private Household Worker
■ Executive Housekeeper
■ Maid
■ Cleaner
■ Street Sweeper
■ Maintenance Repairer
■ Window Cleaner

EARNINGS
■ $11,670 to $19,140 to $25,000

OUTLOOK

■ Employment for this occupation is expected to grow only as fast as the average through 2010, according to the U.S. Department of Labor. The janitorial field is an easy one to enter, since little training or education is required. Relatively high turnover is expected. Businesses providing janitorial and cleaning services on a contract basis are expected to be among the fastest-growing employers of these workers.

FOR MORE INFORMATION

For information on careers and training in the janitorial services field, contact:

Cleaning and Maintenance Management Online
National Trade Publications
13 Century Hill Drive
Latham, NY 12110
518-783-1281
http://www.cmmonline.com

For information about certification programs in housekeeping, contact:

International Executive Housekeepers Association, Inc.
1001 Eastwind Drive, Suite 301
Westerville, OH 43081-3361
800-200-6342
excel@ieha.org
http://www.ieha.org

For information on the cleaning industry, training programs, and how to start a cleaning business, contact:

Janitor USA
Cornerstone Publications Inc.
650 East Walnut Street, Suite A
PO Box 955
Elizabeth, CO 80107
303-646-5388
http://www.janitorusa.com

■ Licensed Practical Nurse

A licensed practical nurse (LPN) provides bedside care for those who are sick, injured, convalescent, and disabled. They usually work on a health care team under the supervision of a physician or registered nurse. In some nursing homes or assisted-living situations, LPNs may be responsible for directing or supervising other health care workers. Tasks usually include monitoring vital signs, treating bedsores, preparing for and giving injections and enemas, applying dressings and ice packs, inserting and monitoring catheters, and monitoring patient reaction to medications. Other tasks include collecting samples for testing; conducting routine lab tests; feeding and turning patients; assisting patients with dressing, bathing, and personal hygiene tasks; recording food and fluid intake; charting; and providing emotional support.

MAY BE GOOD FOR YOU NOW IF YOU
■ Desire to engage in direct patient care

■ Have a strong desire to help people who are sick, injured, and disabled

■ Plan to become a registered nurse and want to become familiar with the nursing team experience

HELPFUL PERSONAL TRAITS
■ Patient

■ Compassionate

■ Warm and friendly

■ Able to make keen observations and sound judgments

■ Physical stamina

■ Good vision

■ Manual dexterity

■ Ability to react quickly

VALUE TO YOUR CAREER DEVELOPMENT
■ May help realize the values of love and helping those in need

■ Satisfaction derived from having helped those who suffer

VALUE TO EMPLOYER/SOCIETY
■ Contributes to relieving pain and suffering as well as providing comfort, relief, and emotional support to patients

- Fills a continuing urgent health care need in America

POSSIBLE DOWNSIDES
- Must be on your feet for long periods of time
- May be susceptible to back injuries from lifting patients
- May be exposed to harmful chemicals, radiation, and infections
- May have to work long, irregular hours
- May have to deal with uncooperative patients

POPULATION GROUPS
- Part-Time/Temporary
- Single Parent
- Volunteer
- General

PREPARATION
- A high school diploma plus approximately one year of intensive training at an accredited state nursing program is required for entry. Programs are offered through community or technical colleges as well as some vocational schools.
- Continuing education courses are recommended to stay abreast of changing procedures and technology

CERTIFICATION
- All 50 states require graduates of a state-approved practical nursing program to take a licensing examination. LPNs may also take the Certification Exam for Practical and Vocational Nurses in Long-Term Care (CEPN-LTC). Contact the National Council of State Boards of Nursing for more information.

RELATED JOBS/TITLES
- Licensed Vocational Nurse
- Practical Nurse
- Paramedic
- Surgical Technologist
- Medical Technician
- Social Service Assistant

EARNINGS
■ $21,520 to $29,440 to $41,800

OUTLOOK
■ According to the *Occupational Outlook Handbook,* jobs for LPNs are projected to grow about as fast as the average through 2010. Traditionally, hospitals have provided the most job opportunities for LPNs. However, this source will provide only a moderate number of openings in the future. Faster-than-average employment growth is predicted for LPNs in nursing homes and home health care agencies. Private medical practices will also be excellent job sources because many medical procedures are now being performed on an outpatient basis in doctors' offices.

FOR MORE INFORMATION
For information on education programs and careers, contact the following organizations:

American Association of Colleges of Nursing
One Dupont Circle, NW, Suite 530
Washington, DC 20036
202-463-6930
http://www.aacn.nche.edu

National Association for Practical Nurse Education and Services
1400 Spring Street, Suite 330
Silver Spring, MD 20910
301-588-2839
napnes@bellatlantic.net

For information on careers and certification, contact the following organization:

National Council of State Boards of Nursing
676 North St. Clair Street, Suite 550
Chicago, IL 60611-2921
312-787-6555
info@ncsbn.org
http://www.ncsbn.org

For career information, contact the following organizations:

National Federation of Licensed Practical Nurses, Inc.
893 US Highway 70 West, Suite 202
Garner, NC 27529
800-948-2511
http://www.nflpn.org

National League for Nursing
61 Broadway
New York, NY 10006
800-669-1656
http://www.nln.org

Discover Nursing, sponsored by Johnson & Johnson Health Care Systems, provides information on nursing careers, nursing schools, and scholarships:

Discover Nursing
http://www.discovernursing.com

■ Line Installer

A line installer is a telecommunications worker who installs, maintains, and replaces telephone and cable lines and equipment for commercial and residential sites. Among the duties performed are constructing utility poles, towers, and underground trenches. Other work includes stringing, setting, attaching, bolting, or clamping cable or electrical lines; operating hydraulic buckets; checking transmission signals; replacing transformers, breakers, switches, and fuses; splicing and joining wires and cables; and providing customer service.

MAY BE GOOD FOR YOU NOW IF YOU

■ Are comfortable working at heights

■ Have a background in electrical work

■ Are able to climb and lift heavy and awkward objects

■ Enjoy working outdoors

HELPFUL PERSONAL TRAITS

■ Good in math (algebra and trigonometry)

■ In good physical shape

■ Good communication skills

■ Good at understanding maps and schematic drawings

■ Able to distinguish color

■ Good eye-hand coordination

VALUE TO YOUR CAREER DEVELOPMENT

■ Can help meet the values of adventure, achievement, skill, and helping others

■ Satisfaction derived from knowing your work has a positive impact on the lives of people after you have assisted in restoring power to an area

VALUE TO EMPLOYER/SOCIETY

■ Work restores vital services to save many people and businesses from significant loss and emotional stress

■ Can contribute to the convenience, comfort, and safety of millions in America

POSSIBLE DOWNSIDES
- Risk of falls and injuries
- Danger of electrical shock or electrocution
- May have to work in bad weather
- May have to work long and irregular hours during emergencies

POPULATION GROUPS
- General

PREPARATION
- May be able to enter as ground worker or helper and then advance to line installer
- Usually learn on the job through employer training programs
- Experience in electrical or electronics work is helpful
- Employers may give pre-employment tests to determine verbal, mechanical, and mathematical aptitudes; some employers test applicants for stamina, balance, coordination, and strength
- Workers who drive a company vehicle need a driver's license and a good driving record

CERTIFICATION
- The Society of Cable Television Engineers offers a voluntary installer certification program to establish minimum skill requirements for installers and technicians in the cable telecommunications industry.

RELATED JOBS/TITLES
- Line Mechanic
- Power Line Installer
- Cable Installer
- Electrician
- Electrical and Electronic Installer

EARNINGS
- $25,710 to $45,780 to $63,130

OUTLOOK
- The U.S. Department of Labor anticipates that employment growth for line installers and cable splicers will be faster than the

average through 2010, although the trend will vary among industries. For example, for those working specifically for electric companies, employment will grow more slowly than the average, while those working as telephone or cable television installers are predicted to have faster-than-average job growth.

FOR MORE INFORMATION

To learn about issues affecting jobs in telecommunications, visit the following Web site:

Communications Workers of America
501 Third Street, NW
Washington, DC 20001-2797
202-434-1100
http://www.cwa-union.org

For information about union representation, contact:

International Brotherhood of Electrical Workers
1125 15th Street, NW
Washington, DC 20005
202-833-7000
http://www.ibew.org

For information on careers and the cable industry, contact:

National Cable and Telecommunications Association
1724 Massachusetts Avenue, NW
Washington, DC 20036
202-775-3550
http://www.ncta.com

For information on training seminars and certification, contact:

Society for Cable Telecommunications Engineers
140 Philips Road
Exton, PA 19341
800-542-5040
http://www.scte.org

For information about conferences, special programs, and membership, contact:

Women in Cable and Telecommunications
230 West Monroe, Suite 2630
Chicago, IL 60606
312-634-2330
http://www.wict.org

■ Materials Moving Worker

A materials moving worker moves materials of all types over short distances as well as performing other unskilled labor. Work varies greatly depending on the setting, but usually includes loading and unloading and moving materials to and from storage and production sites and loading docks, vehicles, ships, and containers. Items moved may include raw materials and finished products. Other common tasks are receiving, sorting, preparing materials, packing, bagging, wrapping, and stacking.

MAY BE GOOD FOR YOU NOW IF YOU
■ Desire part-time, temporary, or seasonal work

■ Have limited skills but enjoy manual work

■ Want to work outdoors

■ Want to do work that helps keep you in good physical shape

HELPFUL PERSONAL TRAITS
■ Physically strong and in good health

■ Good at hands-on activities

■ Friendly and polite

■ Industrious

■ Good at following instructions

■ Courageous

VALUE TO YOUR CAREER DEVELOPMENT
■ Can help meet the values of health, achievement, and loyalty

■ Satisfaction derived from knowing your efforts are appreciated by employers and customers who ship and receive goods undamaged

VALUE TO EMPLOYER/SOCIETY
■ Enables millions of goods and products to be successfully transported

■ Provides a vital link in the vast network of packing and transporting items to individuals and businesses across the country

POSSIBLE DOWNSIDES
■ May have to work outdoors in poor weather

■ May involve heavy lifting, carrying, and bending

- May have to work at heights
- May be exposed to fumes, loud noises, and other dangerous conditions
- Earnings may be low

POPULATION GROUPS

- Part-Time/Temporary
- Limited Disabled
- Ex-Offenders
- General

PREPARATION

- Requires no formal education or prior work experience
- Job tasks are learned informally on the job
- Employers may require a physical exam for more physically challenging jobs
- Some employers require a drug test before hiring

CERTIFICATION

- Certification is not usually associated with this occupation

RELATED JOBS/TITLES

- Loading Worker
- Stevedore
- Construction Laborer
- Agricultural Worker
- Refuse Worker
- Baggage Handler

EARNINGS

- $12,980 to $18,810 to $30,880

OUTLOOK

- According to the *Occupational Outlook Handbook* (*OOH*), jobs for materials moving workers are projected to increase about as fast as the average through 2010. Job openings should be numerous because the occupation is very large and turnover is high. The *OOH* reports that employment is expected to grow rapidly in temporary help organizations as more firms contract out material moving services.

FOR MORE INFORMATION
For information on careers and certification in the moving and storage industry, contact:

American Moving and Storage Association
1611 Duke Street
Alexandria, VA 22314
703-683-7410
amconf@amconf.org
http://www.promover.org

For further information on stevedoring occupations, contact the following unions:

International Longshoremen's Association
17 Battery Place, Room 930
New York, NY 10004
212-425-1200
http://www.ilaunion.org

International Longshore and Warehouse Union
1188 Franklin Street, Fourth Floor
San Francisco, CA 94109
415-775-0533
http://www.ilwu.org

Information on safety and training requirements is available from:

U.S. Department of Labor
Occupational Safety and Health Administration (OSHA)
200 Constitution Avenue, NW
Washington, DC 20210
http://www.osha.gov

■ Meatcutter

Meatcutters work in retail establishments or meat processing plants. Tasks vary depending on the setting but usually include most or all of the following: washing and cutting large sections of meat; cutting meats into steaks and chops; shaping and tying roasts; curing meat; grinding beef; wrapping, packaging, and labeling meats; arranging meat for display and preparing spread cuts; cleaning work areas; sharpening knives; and answering customer questions. Some of the tools and equipment used includes knives, scales, slicers, meat grinders, power cutters, conveyors, and band saws.

MAY BE GOOD FOR YOU NOW IF YOU
■ Enjoy working in cool environments
■ Enjoy physical work
■ Want to manage or own a meat market
■ Are familiar with meat cutting

HELPFUL PERSONAL TRAITS
■ Good health and personal hygiene habits
■ Good eye-hand coordination and manual dexterity
■ Able to distinguish colors
■ Good listening skills
■ Friendly
■ Careful and conscientious

VALUE TO YOUR CAREER DEVELOPMENT
■ May help meet values of skills, achievement, and serving others
■ Can help develop perseverance in an environment that is not always comfortable

VALUE TO EMPLOYER/SOCIETY
■ Prepares meat in a way that is appealing to encourage purchases
■ Provides a source of protein and other nutrition for American diets
■ Contributes to the culinary delight of millions each year

POSSIBLE DOWNSIDES
- High rate of injuries, particularly slips and falls, and sickness due to accidents and infections
- Often work in cold, messy conditions, sometimes with unpleasant odors
- Must be on your feet for long periods
- Low wages

POPULATION GROUPS
- Part-Time/Temporary
- General

PREPARATION
- Usually requires little or no prior training
- Skills are learned on the job, including cutting techniques and food safety procedures
- A health certificate may be required

CERTIFICATION
- Certification is not usually associated with this job.

RELATED JOBS/TITLES
- Butcher
- Slaughterer
- Trimmer
- Poultry Cutter
- Fish Cutter
- Meat Packer

EARNINGS
- $13,310 to $16,766 to $23,400

OUTLOOK
- During the past decade the number of meatcutters has slowly declined, and the decline is expected to continue through 2010, according to the U.S. Department of Labor. Meatcutting plants are located near the commercial feedlots of Kansas, Texas, Nebraska, and Oklahoma. The center of the pork industry continues to be in the Midwest, in the states of Illinois, Nebraska,

Minnesota, Iowa, and Michigan. Poultry processing jobs are most likely to be found in the southern and southeastern states, such as Arkansas, Georgia, Alabama, North Carolina, Mississippi, Tennessee, and Virginia, and occasionally in the Atlantic states and California.

FOR MORE INFORMATION

For information on the industry and education resources, contact:

American Association of Meat Processors
PO Box 269
Elizabethtown, PA 17022
717-367-1168
http://www.aamp.com

This organization offers information on industry research, legislative and regulatory affairs, and education programs.

American Meat Institute
1700 North Moore Street, Suite 1600
Arlington, VA 22209
703-841-2400
http://www.meatami.org

This union represents workers in the meat packing industry.

United Food and Commercial Workers Union
1775 K Street, NW
Washington, DC 20006
202-223-3111
http://www.ufcw.org

■ Military Worker, Enlisted

Military workers serve in the U. S. army, navy, air force, marines, Coast Guard, Air and Army National Guard, or one of the various reserve organizations. Duties vary considerably, and actual responsibilities depend on the area assigned. For example, if in combat, a military worker might operate weapons, fire missiles, operate tanks, fly planes, or drive jeeps. Many military jobs, however, have civilian counterparts, such as constructing and building roads, bridges, and other structures. There are jobs in the areas of engineering science, health care, human services, machine production, transportation mechanics, and administration. Other areas of military work include electrical/electronics equipment repair, computer instrumentation, navigational controls, weapons maintenance, communications, and weapons systems. As you can see, the descriptions of the many jobs and tasks are too extensive to include.

MAY BE GOOD FOR YOU NOW IF YOU
■ Have taken high school ROTC

■ Have family members who have previously served and have encouraged you to join

■ Have always wanted to be in the military and believe you could make a positive contribution

HELPFUL PERSONAL TRAITS
■ Courageous

■ Quick-thinking

■ Excellent health and physical condition

■ Respond well in emergencies and under stress

■ Competitive

■ Good at following orders

VALUE TO YOUR CAREER DEVELOPMENT
■ May help meet the values of loyalty, achievement, commitment, power, justice, freedom, helping others, and recognition

■ Satisfaction derived from helping defend your country against any who would seek to harm Americans and their interests, whether it be on the front lines or in a support position

VALUE TO EMPLOYER/SOCIETY
- Helps to ensure freedom and the American way of life
- Contributes to both national and world security and stability
- Commitment to serve reflects your willingness to pay the ultimate price, if necessary, for the protection and safety of all Americans

POSSIBLE DOWNSIDES
- Requires years of commitment
- Long period of time away from loved ones may cause loneliness
- Can be exposed to great danger during both peacetime and war
- Could suffer serious injury or death in the line of duty

POPULATION GROUPS
- Job Complement
- General

PREPARATION
- Must be between 17 and 35 years of age, have a high school diploma or GED, be a U.S. citizen, be drug- and felony-free, and have permanent residence in this country
- Must pass a written and physical examination
- For specialized jobs such as engineering, a bachelor's degree or higher is required
- Hard work and appropriate behavior can lead to advancement

CERTIFICATION
- Certification or licensing depends on the job you have. Pharmacists in the military, for example, must hold a license, the same as civilian pharmacists. However, it is important to note that the military does not offer certification or licensing for many jobs that require credentials in the civilian sector. If you are interested in receiving training in the military for a certain job and plan to transfer your skills to an equivalent job in the civilian sector, you will need to do some research to determine what, if any, additional training and/or certification or licensing you will need in the civilian workforce.

RELATED JOBS/TITLES

- Peace Corps Volunteer
- Government Worker
- Police Officer
- Security Guard

EARNINGS

- The U.S. Congress sets the pay scales for the military after hearing recommendations from the president. The pay for equivalent grades is the same in all services (that is, anyone with a grade of E-4, for example, will have the same basic pay whether in the army, navy, marines, air force, or Coast Guard). In addition to basic pay, personnel who frequently and regularly participate in combat may earn hazardous duty pay. Other special allowances include special duty pay and foreign duty pay. Earnings start relatively low but increase on a fairly regular basis as individuals advance in rank. When reviewing earnings, it is important to keep in mind that members of the military receive free housing, food, and health care—items that civilians typically pay for themselves.

  According to the Defense Finance and Accounting Service, the basic monthly pay for an enlisted member just starting out at a grade of E-1 was $964.80 in 2001. This would make for a yearly salary of approximately $11,577. An enlisted member with an E-5 grade and more than four years' experience earned monthly basic pay of $1,791, or approximately $20,412 yearly. At the top grade of E-9, a person with more than 12 years' experience made $3,197.40 per month, or approximately $38,368 per year.

OUTLOOK

- Career opportunities in the military services are widespread. Today each service branch is aiming to function on a "steady state." This means every year each branch needs enough recruits to replace those leaving the service. According to the U.S. Department of Labor, approximately 365,000 new enlistees and officers must join annually to fill vacated spots. In recent years some branches, such as the Navy, have fallen short of meeting their recruitment goals, and opportunities in these branches are even more plentiful than the average. While political and economic conditions will have an influence on the military's duties and employment outlook, it is a fact that the country will always need the armed forces, both for defense and to protect its interests and citizens around the world.

FOR MORE INFORMATION

Each of the following services publishes handbooks, fact sheets, and pamphlets describing entrance requirements, training, advancement possibilities, and other aspects of military careers. For more information, contact the following offices or your local recruiter.

Marine Corps Recruiting Command
800-MARINES
http://www.marines.com

Navy Recruiting Command
800-USA-NAVY
http://www.navy.com

United States Air Force Recruiting Service, Headquarters
800-423-USAF
http://www.airforce.com

United States Army Recruiting Command, Headquarters
800-USA-ARMY
http://www.goarmy.com

United States Coast Guard Recruiting
800-GET-USCG
http://www.uscg.mil

To view the Military Career Guide Online, which contains information on opportunities in all branches of the service, visit the following Web site:

Military Career Guide Online
http://www.militarycareers.com

■ Nursing Aide

A nursing aide performs various routine tasks for patients in hospitals, nursing homes, residential care centers, and other medical facilities. They work under the supervision of nursing and medical staff. Duties may include answering call bells; serving meals; making beds; helping patients eat, dress, and bathe; delivering messages; and transporting or escorting patients. Other responsibilities may include setting up equipment, arranging rooms, reporting concerns to other health team members, and assisting patients in and out of bed and with walking.

MAY BE GOOD FOR YOU NOW IF YOU
- Enjoy developing relationships with others
- Have a genuine desire to help those who are sick or injured
- Want to volunteer in a health care setting
- Plan to become a health professional

HELPFUL PERSONAL TRAITS
- Good health and physical stamina
- Warm and friendly
- Gentle and compassionate
- Hard worker
- Discreet
- Team player
- Good communication skills
- Patient

VALUE TO YOUR CAREER DEVELOPMENT
- Can help meet the values of love, serving others, and recognition
- Satisfaction derived from knowing you have helped others

VALUE TO EMPLOYER/SOCIETY
- Helps to fill a critical need for primary care, particularly in nursing/assisted living facilities
- Plays an important role on the health care team

POSSIBLE DOWNSIDES

- Must be on your feet for long periods
- Could be emotionally stressful
- Danger of contracting infectious diseases
- May have heavy workload and some unpleasant tasks
- May need to lift and move large people, exposing you to risks of back injury

POPULATION GROUPS

- Part-Time/Temporary
- Single Parent
- Volunteer
- General

PREPARATION

- A high school diploma or previous work experience is not required
- Duties are learned on the job
- Some community colleges and vocational schools offer short training courses

CERTIFICATION

- Some states require nursing aides to be certified no matter where they work. Nursing aides who work in nursing homes are required to undergo special training. Nursing homes can hire inexperienced workers as nursing aides or assistants, but these workers must have at least 75 hours of training and pass a competency evaluation program within four months of being hired. Those who fulfill these requirements are then certified.

RELATED JOBS/TITLES

- Nursing Assistant
- Hospital Attendant
- Geriatric Aide
- Medical Assistant

EARNINGS

- $13,480 to $18,500 to $26,390

OUTLOOK

■ According to the *Occupational Outlook Handbook,* jobs for nursing aides are projected to grow faster than the average through 2010. Because of the physical and emotional demands of the job, and because of the lack of advancement opportunities, there is a high employee turnover rate. More nursing aides will be required as government and private agencies develop more programs to assist people with disabilities, dependent people, and the increasing aging population.

FOR MORE INFORMATION

For additional information on nurse assistant careers and training, contact:

Career Nurse Assistants' Program, Inc.
3577 Easton Road
Norton, OH 44203-5661
330-825-9342
Info-CNA@cna-network.org
http://www.cna-network.org

Discover Nursing, sponsored by Johnson & Johnson Health Care Systems, provides information on nursing careers, nursing schools, and scholarships:

Discover Nursing
http://www.discovernursing.com

■ Occupational Therapist Aide

Occupational therapist aides work under the direct supervision of
an occupational therapist or occupational therapist assistant. They
help people who have mental, physical, emotional, or developmental impairments to adapt to their living environments.
Occupational therapist aides prepare materials and equipment
used during the treatment carried out by occupational therapists
and their assistants. Other tasks are clerical, such as answering
phones, ordering and replenishing supplies, scheduling appointments, and completing various types of paperwork.

MAY BE GOOD FOR YOU NOW IF YOU

■ Want to work part-time, evenings, or weekends

■ Would like to volunteer

■ Like to help those who have disabilities

■ Need experience in this field because you plan to become an
  occupational therapist or an occupational therapist assistant

HELPFUL PERSONAL TRAITS

■ A team player

■ Physical stamina

■ Compassionate

■ Good health

■ Patient

■ Strong communication skills

■ Honest

■ Tactful and discreet

VALUE TO YOUR CAREER DEVELOPMENT

■ Can help meet the values of helping others, love, and health

■ Satisfaction derived from recognition received from appreciative
  patients

VALUE TO EMPLOYER/SOCIETY

■ Helps to meet a critical need of a growing number of Americans

■ Contributes to helping people with disabilities perform more
  day-to-day activities

POSSIBLE DOWNSIDES
- May be required to lift, kneel, stoop, and stand for long periods

POPULATION GROUPS
- Part-Time/Temporary
- Volunteer
- General

PREPARATION
- A high school diploma is required
- Employers provide on-the-job training

CERTIFICATION
- Certification is not usually associated with this occupation (To become an occupational therapist assistant, you must complete an associate's degree or certificate program; some states also require licensing.)

RELATED JOBS/TITLES
- Physical Therapist Aide
- Dental Assistant
- Medical Assistant
- Pharmacy Technician
- Nursing Aide

EARNINGS
- $14,370 to $20,710 to $35,900

OUTLOOK
- According to the *Occupational Outlook Handbook,* jobs for occupational therapist aides are projected to grow much faster than the average through 2010. Growth will stem from the increased number of elderly people, who will need the kinds of services occupational therapy provides.

FOR MORE INFORMATION

For additional information on careers, education, and news related to the field, contact AOTA:

American Occupational Therapy Association (AOTA)
4720 Montgomery Lane
PO Box 31220
Bethesda, MD 20824-1220
301-652-2682
http://www.aota.org

For information on certification, contact:

National Board for Certification in Occupational Therapy
The Eugene B. Casey Building
800 South Frederick Avenue, Suite 200
Gaithersburg, MD 20877-4150
301-990-7979
http://www.nbcot.org

■ Office Clerk

An office clerk works in an office setting and performs a variety of routine tasks, such as filing; counting; keyboarding and data entry into computers; stapling; operating photocopiers, fax machines, printers, and scanners; collecting and collating materials; stuffing envelopes; proofreading; locating documents; and answering phones. Some office clerks fill orders, replenish shelves, take inventory, and perform other record-keeping tasks. They may also type and mail invoices and sort payments as they come in, keep payroll records, or take inventories. They run errands and deliver messages from one office worker to another or from office workers to people outside the company.

MAY BE GOOD FOR YOU NOW IF YOU
■ Have worked in an office before and enjoy it

■ Want part-time or temporary work

■ Want to learn general office skills by volunteering

HELPFUL PERSONAL TRAITS
■ Don't mind doing repetitive tasks

■ Accurate

■ Detail-oriented

■ Good communication skills

■ Good math skills

■ Dependable

■ Flexible

■ Team player

■ Good at following directions

■ Proficient in spelling, grammar, and editing

VALUE TO YOUR CAREER DEVELOPMENT
■ Can help meet the values of helping others, achievement, and skill

■ Satisfaction derived from being a part of a team effort and completing a task together

VALUE TO EMPLOYER/SOCIETY
- Provides support to other office workers
- Frees upper-level staff to perform more complex tasks

POSSIBLE DOWNSIDES
- Low wages
- Can be monotonous and boring
- May rarely get positive recognition

POPULATION GROUPS
- Part-Time/Temporary
- Single Parent
- Senior Citizen
- General

PREPARATION
- Most employers prefer a high school diploma
- Computer training, word processing skills, and business courses are helpful
- Basic math skills are required
- Legible handwriting is important

CERTIFICATION
- Certification is not usually associated with this occupation

RELATED JOBS/TITLES
- Records Clerk
- Information Clerk
- Payroll Clerk
- File Clerk
- Secretary

EARNINGS
- $13,650 to $21,130 to $33,050

OUTLOOK
- According to the *Occupational Outlook Handbook,* jobs for office clerks are projected to grow about as fast as the average through

2010. There will be many jobs available due to the size of this field and a high turnover rate. The strongest demand for administrative staff is expected to be in the technology, financial services, construction, and manufacturing industries.

FOR MORE INFORMATION

For information on seminars, conferences, and industry news, contact:

National Association of Executive Secretaries and Administrative Assistants
900 South Washington Street, Suite G-13
Falls Church, VA 22046
703-237-8616
http://www.naesaa.com

For free office career and salary information, visit the following Web site:

OfficeTeam
http://www.officeteam.com

■ Painter

A painter's job consists of the application of paint, stain, or other finishes to surfaces inside and outside buildings and structures of all types. Tasks include selecting and purchasing the appropriate finish, preparing surfaces by patching holes and cracks, sanding, and applying primer. Painters also mix paint; match colors; strip old finishes; tape edges; apply finishes with brushes, rollers, or sprayers; clean equipment and tools; and make price quotes. In addition to paint-application tools, painters use pails, trays, drop cloths, ladders, scaffolds, ropes, cables, and roof hooks.

MAY BE GOOD FOR YOU NOW IF YOU
■ Desire to work during the summer

■ Enjoy painting

■ Are looking for a way to earn money for college

■ Like climbing and working in high places

HELPFUL PERSONAL TRAITS
■ Physical stamina

■ Good eye-hand coordination

■ Good color sense

■ Neat and efficient

■ Able to work alone as well as on a team

■ Able to plan and organize

■ Respectful of others' property

VALUE TO YOUR CAREER DEVELOPMENT
■ Can help meet the values of esthetics, physical appearance, and achievement

■ Satisfaction derived from seeing improvement in the physical appearance of a property

VALUE TO EMPLOYER/SOCIETY
■ Contributes to the maintenance and attractiveness of residential and commercial property, thus helping to improve property values

■ Helps to preserve structures from weather damage

POSSIBLE DOWNSIDES
- Requires bending, climbing, stretching, and standing
- At risk for slips or falls from ladders, scaffolding, or steep roofs
- Exposure to strong fumes and may require wearing a mask
- Can be messy

POPULATION GROUPS
- Part-Time/Temporary
- Ex-Offender
- Limited Disabled
- General

PREPARATION
- No formal education is required for entry
- Most learn skills on the job as a helper to an experienced painter or through an apprenticeship

CERTIFICATION
- Certification is not usually associated with this occupation

RELATED JOBS/TITLES
- Paper Hanger
- Decorator
- Plasterer
- Drywall Installer
- Carpenter

EARNINGS
- $17,800 to $27,250 to $46,570

OUTLOOK
- According to the *Occupational Outlook Handbook,* jobs for painters are projected to grow about as fast as the average through 2010. Turnover is very high in this trade.

FOR MORE INFORMATION

For additional information about becoming a painter or paperhanger, contact the following organizations:

International Union of Painters and Allied Trades
1750 New York Avenue, NW
Washington, DC 20006
http://www.iupat.org

National Association of Home Builders
1201 15th Street, NW
Washington, DC 20005
800-368-5242
http://www.nahb.com

Painting and Decorating Contractors of America
3913 Old Lee Highway, 2nd Floor
Fairfax, VA 22030
703-359-0800
http://www.pdca.org

■ Payroll Clerk

A payroll clerk oversees and maintains employee time reports and computes wages and deductions. Specific tasks may include screening time cards, verifying hours worked, data entry, making adjustments and corrections, distributing checks, and answering inquiries about benefits.

MAY BE GOOD FOR YOU NOW IF YOU
■ Like to work with numbers

■ Have worked as a treasurer or cashier in the past

■ Plan to study banking, finance, or accounting

HELPFUL PERSONAL TRAITS
■ Respectful of confidential information

■ Discreet

■ Trustworthy

■ Organized

■ Proficient in business math or accounting

■ Good computer skills

■ Conscientious

■ Good communication skills

VALUE TO YOUR CAREER DEVELOPMENT
■ Can help meet the values of skill, morality, service, and honesty

■ Satisfaction derived from being efficient and ensuring that employees are appropriately paid

VALUE TO EMPLOYER/SOCIETY
■ Has key role in making sure employees are paid accurately and on time each pay period

■ Accuracy and efficiency helps both employers and employees minimize or avoid potential financial hardships caused by delays in pay or benefits

POSSIBLE DOWNSIDES
■ May spend long periods of time sitting at your work station

■ Pressure to meet deadlines can be stressful

POPULATION GROUPS
- Single Parent
- General

PREPARATION
- A high school diploma is usually the minimum requirement
- Most skills are learned on the job
- Basic math skills are important
- Word processing and computer skills are helpful

CERTIFICATION
- Certification is not usually associated with this occupation

RELATED JOBS/TITLES
- Financial Clerk
- Auditing Clerk
- Accounting Clerk
- Bookkeeper
- Cashier

EARNINGS
- $18,420 to $27,180 to $40,190

OUTLOOK
- According to the *Occupational Outlook Handbook,* jobs for pay-roll clerks are projected to grow more slowly than the average through 2010. Despite lack of growth, there will be numerous replacement job openings, since the turnover rate in this occupation is high. Opportunities for temporary work should increase.

FOR MORE INFORMATION
For information on accredited educational programs, contact:

Association to Advance Collegiate Schools of Business
600 Emerson Road, Suite 300
St. Louis, MO 63141-6762
314-872-8481
http://www.aacsb.edu

For more information on women in accounting, contact:

Educational Foundation for Women in Accounting
PO Box 1925
Southeastern, PA 19399-1925
610-407-9229
info@efwa.org
http://www.efwa.org

For information on seminars, conferences, and news on the industry, contact:

National Association of Executive Secretaries and Administrative Assistants
900 South Washington Street, Suite G-13
Falls Church, VA 22046
703-237-8616
http://www.naesaa.com

For free office career and salary information, visit the following Web site:

OfficeTeam
http://www.officeteam.com

■ Postal Service Worker

A postal service worker collects and sorts mail and waits on customers who have postal service needs. Tasks include weighing envelopes and packages, taping packages, responding to customer inquiries, providing instructions, selling postage stamps, and receiving money and making change. Postal service workers lift and move containers; operate cash registers, letter-sorting machines, and other office equipment; and perform various clerical tasks. Some postal service workers are mail carriers and deliver mail and packages to residents and businesses either on foot or by vehicle. Mail carriers may have to drive or operate nonmotorized equipment.

MAY BE GOOD FOR YOU NOW IF YOU

■ Enjoy working with the public

■ Want to do a lot of walking and stay in good physical shape

■ Don't mind lifting and carrying

HELPFUL PERSONAL TRAITS

■ Accurate and detail-oriented

■ Finger dexterity

■ Work well on a team as well as independently

■ Physically fit and healthy

■ Good communication skills

■ Good memory

■ Responsible

■ Dedicated

VALUE TO YOUR CAREER DEVELOPMENT

■ Can help to meet the values of health, service to others, loyalty, and achievement

■ Satisfaction derived from providing a service that people depend on daily

VALUE TO EMPLOYER/SOCIETY

■ Contributes to maintaining a primary method of communication and information for millions of Americans

■ Receiving and sending mail can help maintain business communications and transactions

POSSIBLE DOWNSIDES

- Must stand and walk for long periods, sometimes in bad weather
- May have to lift and carry heavy loads
- Can be stressful during peak mailing periods, such as during holiday seasons
- May be threatened or bitten by unsupervised animals
- May have to deal with unhappy or uncooperative customers

POPULATION GROUPS

- Part-Time/Temporary
- General

PREPARATION

- Must be 18 years old
- Must have a driver's license
- Must pass a written civil-service exam before entry into U.S. Postal Service jobs
- Must be able to lift 70 lbs.

CERTIFICATION

- Certification is not usually associated with this occupation

RELATED JOBS/TITLES

- Postal Clerk
- Mail Carrier
- Mail Sorter
- Mail Processor
- Counter Clerk
- Rental Clerk
- Shipping and Receiving Clerk

EARNINGS

- Postal clerks: $31,980 to $39,010 to $43,590
- Mail carriers: $26,140 to $38,420 to $44,040
- Sorters/processors: $18,940 to $32,080 to $42,570

OUTLOOK

■ According to the *Occupational Outlook Handbook,* jobs for postal service workers are projected to decline through 2010. The United States Postal Service expects mail volume to decrease primarily because of the increased competition from other delivery services, including email. Postal clerk jobs will decline because of technological developments, including automation and electronic sorting and canceling devices.

FOR MORE INFORMATION

The following union organizations offer information about employment:

American Postal Workers Union
Research and Education Department
1300 L Street, NW, Suite 525
Washington, DC 20005
http://www.apwu.org

National Postal Mail Handlers Union
1101 Connecticut Avenue, NW, Suite 500
Washington, DC 20036
http://www.npmhu.org

For information about eligibility and qualifying examinations for the U.S. Postal Service, consult your local post office or state employment service. For general information on postal employment, contact:

U.S. Postal Service
Headquarters Personnel Division
475 L'Enfant Plaza, SW, Room 1813
Washington, DC 20260-4261
800-474-7195
http://www.usps.gov/hrisp/ (for job listings)

The following commercial delivery companies also offer employment opportunities:

Airborne Freight Corporation
3101 Western Avenue
PO Box 662
Seattle, WA 98111-0662
http://www2.airborne.com/HRWeb/

Federal Express
PO Box 727
Memphis, TN 38194
901-395-4555
http://www.fedex.com/us/careers/

United Parcel Service of America
Human Resources
55 Glenlake Parkway, NE
Atlanta, GA 30328
888-967-5877
http://www.upsjobs.com

■ Physical Therapist Aide

A physical therapist aide works under the direct supervision of a physical therapist or a physical therapist assistant. The PTA is part of the physical therapy team and assists other team members in the effort to increase the mobility and relieve the pain and suffering of patients who have temporary or permanent disabilities. Duties usually include cleaning, organizing, and preparing the treatment area for patient therapy; helping patients move to and from treatment areas; pushing patients in wheelchairs; and providing physical support when needed. Other tasks are clerical and include answering calls, ordering supplies, and completing insurance forms and other paperwork.

MAY BE GOOD FOR YOU NOW IF YOU

■ Have a strong desire to work with people with disabilities

■ Want to do volunteer work in this area

■ Plan to become a physical therapist or physical therapist assistant

HELPFUL PERSONAL TRAITS

■ Physical stamina

■ Good health

■ Good communication skills

■ Gentle and compassionate

■ Patient

■ Honest

■ Tactful and discreet

■ Team player

VALUE TO YOUR CAREER DEVELOPMENT

■ Can help meet the values of helping others, love, health, and achievement

■ Satisfaction derived from knowing you are helping to relieve the pain of others

■ Recognition received from those who are appreciative of services effectively rendered, including patients and other members of the physical therapy team

VALUE TO EMPLOYER/SOCIETY
■ Helps to meet critical health care needs of a growing number of Americans

■ Can help increase the mobility and emotional well-being of the elderly and people with disabilities

■ Can help in the effort to relieve discomfort and pain of others, as well as to prevent more serious injury

POSSIBLE DOWNSIDES
■ Can be physically demanding, requiring a lot of bending, kneeling, stooping, and standing

■ Low pay

POPULATION GROUPS
■ Part-Time/Temporary

■ Single Parent

■ Volunteer

■ General

■ Limited Disabled

PREPARATION
■ A high school diploma is usually required for entry

■ Training is usually provided on the job

■ Advancement to physical therapist assistant requires an associate's degree from an accredited program

CERTIFICATION
■ Certification is not usually associated with this occupation Physical therapist assistants, however, must be registered, certified, or licensed in more than 40 states.

RELATED JOBS/TITLES
■ Physical Therapist Assistant

■ Occupational Therapist Aide

■ Dental Assistant

■ Medical Assistant

EARNINGS
■ $14,590 to $19,670 to $28,800

OUTLOOK

■ According to the *Occupational Outlook Handbook,* jobs for physical therapist aides are projected to grow much faster than the average through 2010. Demand for rehabilitation services is expected to continue to grow much more rapidly than the average for all occupations, and the rate of turnover among workers is relatively high.

FOR MORE INFORMATION

For additional education and career information, contact:

American Physical Therapy Association
1111 North Fairfax Street
Alexandria, VA 22314-1488
800-999-2782
http://www.apta.org

■ Receptionist

A receptionist provides first-contact services for organizations, companies, and agencies. Tasks usually include greeting visitors, managing telephone calls, taking and relaying messages, responding to inquiries, giving directions, making appointments, and providing information. Some receptionists have record-keeping responsibilities, use computers, and operate printers and fax machines.

MAY BE GOOD FOR YOU NOW IF YOU

- Are good at working with people in public settings
- Like to assist and direct others
- Enjoy making a positive impression on others
- Desire to work part-time
- Like to work in a neat and attractive environment

HELPFUL PERSONAL TRAITS

- Warm, friendly, and outgoing
- Good at doing multiple tasks simultaneously
- Patient
- Organized and neat
- Clear, pleasant voice and a poised, professional manner
- Able to work effectively with individuals of different backgrounds, ages, ethnicities, etc.

VALUE TO YOUR CAREER DEVELOPMENT

- May help meet personal values of recognition, helping others, and love
- May meet need for people contact

VALUE TO EMPLOYER/SOCIETY

- Presentation and behavior can have significant impact on the success or failure of an organization or company; in some cases, first impressions can help to generate or lose revenues

POSSIBLE DOWNSIDES

- Low wages
- May not receive deserved recognition

■ May have to work with difficult people

POPULATION GROUPS
■ Part-Time/Temporary

■ Single Parent

■ Volunteer

■ General

PREPARATION
■ No formal education required

■ Tasks are usually learned on the job

■ Courses in business procedures, office machine operation, keyboarding, computers, business math, English, and public speaking are helpful

CERTIFICATION
■ Certificate programs may be available at some vocational schools and community colleges

RELATED JOBS/TITLES
■ Admitting Clerk

■ Hotel Desk Clerk

■ Information Dispatcher

■ Bank Teller

■ Reservation Agent

■ Loan Clerk

EARNINGS
■ $13,860 to $20,040 to $29,000

OUTLOOK
■ Employment for receptionists is expected to grow faster than the average through 2010, according to the *Occupational Outlook Handbook*. Many openings will occur due to the occupation's high turnover rate. Opportunities will be best for those with wide clerical skills and work experience. Opportunities should be especially good in rapid services industries, such as physician's offices, law firms, temporary help agencies, and consulting firms.

FOR MORE INFORMATION

For information on careers, contact:

**International Association of
Administrative Professionals**
10502 NW Ambassador Drive
PO Box 20404
Kansas City, MO 64195-0404
816-891-6600
service@iaap-hq.org
http://www.iaap-hq.org

*For information on seminars, conferences, and news on the industry,
contact:*

**National Association of Executive Secretaries and
Administrative Assistants**
900 South Washington Street, Suite G-13
Falls Church, VA 22046
703-237-8616
http://www.naesaa.com

*For free office career and salary information, visit the following
Web site:*

OfficeTeam
http://www.officeteam.com

■ Refuse/Waste Removal Worker

Refuse/waste removal workers pick up, transport, and unload refuse, garbage, and recyclable materials from designated sites, including households, gardens, and businesses. They may work for a municipal or private contractor and usually collect along assigned routes. Duties include loading and compacting trash and transporting it to landfills or recycling sites. Most of these workers are required to drive a truck and operate dumpster lifts, compactors, and forklift equipment.

MAY BE GOOD FOR YOU NOW IF YOU
■ Like to do hard physical work

■ Can handle the challenge of working with potentially hazardous materials

■ Want experience at the grass-roots level before entering the field of hazardous waste management or other environmental career

HELPFUL PERSONAL TRAITS
■ Good at following directions and understanding street maps

■ Willing to work outdoors in all kinds of weather

■ Physically strong and able to lift up to 100 lbs.

VALUE TO YOUR CAREER DEVELOPMENT
■ May support the values of health, environmental protection, and safety

■ Satisfaction derived from removing waste and hazardous materials that have potential for causing serious health and safety problems if not attended to

VALUE TO EMPLOYER/SOCIETY
■ Collection and removal of waste is a vital public service that helps minimize the possibility of serious health and safety concerns

■ Helps maintain a cleaner, more attractive community and consequently positively affect property values

POSSIBLE DOWNSIDES
■ Exposure to unpleasant odors, fumes, dirt, and grease

■ Susceptible to slips and falls and injuries from heavy lifting

POPULATION GROUPS
- Ex-Offenders
- Limited Disabled

PREPARATION
- No formal education or training is required for entry
- Most employers prefer workers who are at least 18 years old
- Duties are learned on the job
- Workers who drive collection trucks need a commercial driver's license (CDL) and a clean driving record
- Passing a civil service test may be necessary order to work for a city or town

CERTIFICATION
- Certification is not usually associated with this occupation

RELATED JOBS/TITLES
- Garbage Collector
- Trash Collector
- Sanitation Worker
- Roustabout
- Helper

EARNINGS
- $13,980 to $24,610 to $41,380

OUTLOOK
- According to the *Occupational Outlook Handbook,* jobs for refuse/waste removal workers are projected to grow about as fast as the average through 2010. Job turnover is high in this field. Opportunities will be best in heavily populated regions in and near big cities.

FOR MORE INFORMATION

The Environmental Industry Association is an umbrella organization that includes organizations of interest to the solid waste management industry. It publishes two magazines that follow trends and news of the waste industry: Waste Age *and* Recycling Times.

Environmental Industry Association
4301 Connecticut Avenue, NW, Suite 300
Washington, DC 20008
800-424-2869
http://www.envasns.org

This is a national union whose members include refuse collectors:

International Brotherhood of Teamsters, Chauffeurs, Warehousemen and Helpers of America
25 Louisiana Avenue, NW
Washington, DC 20001
202-624-6800
http://www.teamster.org

For information on industry news, publications, and membership, contact:

National Solid Waste Management Association
4301 Connecticut Avenue, NW, Suite 300
Washington, DC 20008
202-624-6800
http://www.nswma.org

■ Retail Salesperson

Retail salespeople work at stores to help customers locate items and provide information that can persuade them to purchase. Tasks vary widely according to what is being sold; high-price items, such as large appliances, furniture, or cars, may require special knowledge and skills. Retail salespeople operate cash registers, handle checks and credit cards, stock shelves, place orders, contact other stores, bag or package purchased items, exchange merchandise, mark prices, prepare displays, take inventory, wrap gifts, and perform housekeeping activities.

MAY BE GOOD FOR YOU NOW IF YOU

■ Want supplemental income

■ Desire part-time, temporary, evening, or weekend work

■ Enjoy working with merchandise and people

■ Want to work in a clean and comfortable environment

HELPFUL PERSONAL TRAITS

■ Outgoing and polite

■ Friendly and cheerful

■ Organized and neat

■ Communicate well with people

■ Self-confident and patient

■ Alert, observant, and quick to help

VALUE TO YOUR CAREER DEVELOPMENT

■ May help to meet values of helping others, recognition, and achievement

■ May help enforce personal traits such as patience and trustworthiness

■ May satisfy needs for socialization, variety, and attractive surroundings

VALUE TO EMPLOYER/SOCIETY

■ Salesperson's behavior and attitude have a significant impact on customers' experiences, which in turn affect future patronage

■ Provides pleasure for shoppers

■ Satisfies consumer demand for products

POSSIBLE DOWNSIDES
- Must be on your feet for long periods
- At times, may have to serve difficult or irate customers
- Low wages and sometimes long hours, including evenings and weekends

POPULATION GROUPS
- Part-Time/Temporary
- Single Parent
- Senior Citizen
- General

PREPARATION
- Usually no formal education is required, but a high school diploma is preferred
- Past experience is helpful if selling high-priced items, and a background check may also be required

CERTIFICATION
- The National Association of Sales Professionals offers certification as a Certified Professional Salesperson (CPSP) upon fulfilling the experience, training, and professional involvement requirements in addition to passing an exam.

  Vocational schools and community colleges may have certification programs in retail sales.

RELATED JOBS/TITLES
- Sales Representative
- Clerk
- Cashier
- Sales Agent
- Buyer

EARNINGS
- $12,180 to $16,670 to $33,000

OUTLOOK
- According to the *Occupational Outlook Handbook,* jobs for retail salespersons should grow about as fast as the average through 2010. Turnover among sales workers is much higher than aver-

age, so many of the expected employment opportunities will stem from the need to replace workers. Demand in the future will be strongest for sales workers who are knowledgeable about particular types of products.

During economic recessions, sales volume and the resulting demand for sales workers generally decline. However, there should continue to be good opportunities for temporary and part-time workers, especially during the holidays.

FOR MORE INFORMATION

For information on certification and employment, contact:

National Association of Sales Professionals
8300 North Hayden Road, Suite 207
Scottsdale, AZ 85258
480-951-4311
http://www.nasp.com

For materials on educational programs in the retail industry, contact:

National Retail Federation
325 7th Street, NW, Suite 1000
Washington, DC 20004
800-673-4692
http://www.nrf.com

■ Roofer

A roofer repairs and installs roofs using various materials, such as wood, tile, asphalt, metal, and iron. Duties can include applying insulation and boarding substance, installing layers of roof felt, spreading molten adhesives and waterproofing substances over roof subsurfaces, and glazing. Other tasks include stapling or nailing shingles to roofs, measuring, cutting, cementing, hot-air welding, caulking, and spraying. Some roofers perform waterproofing and damp-proofing tasks on walls, swimming pools, tanks, and structures other than roofs.

MAY BE GOOD FOR YOU NOW IF YOU
■ Want to do physical work and heavy lifting

■ Enjoy working outdoors

■ Like the challenge of taking risks

■ Are not afraid of heights

■ Need an entry-level job or need to establish a work record

HELPFUL PERSONAL TRAITS
■ Physically strong, healthy, and alert

■ Good eye-hand coordination

■ Good sense of balance

■ Able to follow directions

■ Endurance and stamina

■ Careful

■ Good at measuring and cutting

■ Courageous

VALUE TO YOUR CAREER DEVELOPMENT
■ May help meet the values of achievement, adventure, and skill

■ Satisfaction derived from completing a challenging roof project

VALUE TO EMPLOYER/SOCIETY
■ Helps maintain buildings and other structures

■ Helps ensure safety and comfort of building inhabitants

■ Helps customers avoid significant expense and possible injury due to a water-damaged ceiling or collapsed roof

POSSIBLE DOWNSIDES
- Exposure to dangers of slips, falls, burns from hot substances, and cuts from materials and tools

POPULATION GROUPS
- Ex-Offender
- Part-Time/Temporary
- Limited Disabled
- General

PREPARATION
- No high school diploma is required
- Can enter as a helper and learn skills on the job
- Apprenticeship programs are available
- Basic math and mechanical drawing background is helpful
- Safety training through employers or through OSHA's Outreach Training Program

CERTIFICATION
- Certification is not usually associated with this occupation However, the National Roofing Contractors Association and the Roofing Industry Educational Institute provide various educational resources, including seminars, customized training programs, and certificate programs.

RELATED JOBS/TITLES
- Water Proofer
- Carpenter
- Ceiling/Tile Installer
- Plasterer
- Cement Mason

EARNINGS
- $18,050 to $29,030 to $50,910

OUTLOOK
- According to the *Occupational Outlook Handbook,* jobs for roofers are projected to grow about as fast as the average through 2010. Roofers will always be needed for roof repairs

and replacement, even during economic downturns when construction activity generally decreases. Damp-proofing and water-proofing are expected to provide an increasing proportion of roofing work.

Turnover in this job is high because roofing work is strenuous, hot, and dirty. Many workers consider roofing a temporary job and move into other construction trades. Since roofing is done during the warmer part of the year, job opportunities will probably be best during spring and summer.

FOR MORE INFORMATION

For information on membership benefits and about becoming a professional roofer, contact the following:

National Roofing Contractors Association
10255 West Higgins Road, Suite 600
Rosemont, IL 60018
847-299-9070
nrca@nrca.net
http://nrca.net

United Union of Roofers, Waterproofers and Allied Workers
1660 L Street, NW, Suite 800
Washington, DC 20036
202-463-7663
roofers@unionroofers.com
http://www.unionroofers.com

For information on the Roofing Safety Program and other educational programs, contact:

Roofing Industry Educational Institute
10255 West Higgins Road, Suite 600
Rosemont, IL 60018
847-299-9070
http://nrca.net/riei

■ Security Guard

A security guard protects and secures property, equipment, and people for individuals, companies, or institutions. Duties vary depending on the assignment. Protection can cover such concerns as vandalism, theft, fire, acts of terror, and other illegal activities. Tasks usually include patrolling, door and security checks, inspecting property and equipment, investigating suspicious situations, enforcing rules and laws on property, monitoring alarms, and writing reports.

Other duties may involve crime-prevention activities, interviewing witnesses, and testifying in court. Some security guards perform arrests and issue traffic violations or warnings. Equipment used may include TV cameras, cell phones, two-way radios, keys, and weapons.

MAY BE GOOD FOR YOU NOW IF YOU
■ Want to work part-time

■ Have retired from the military or law enforcement and need to supplement your current income

■ Desire to help meet the need for safety and security

HELPFUL PERSONAL TRAITS
■ Keenly observant and alert

■ Tactful

■ Accurate and detail-oriented

■ Trustworthy and responsible

■ Good health and vision

■ Good judgment

■ Physical stamina

■ Good communication skills

VALUE TO YOUR CAREER DEVELOPMENT
■ Can help meet the values of security, justice, service, safety, and recognition

■ Satisfaction derived from knowing your efforts help to protect property and ensure the safety of people

VALUE TO EMPLOYER/SOCIETY
■ Helps protect workplaces of millions of Americans

■ Since the September 11, 2001, terrorist attacks, the social and economic benefits of having high-quality security have never been valued as much as they are now

POSSIBLE DOWNSIDES
■ Possible danger from physical attack
■ May have to work in poor weather
■ May suffer boredom from monotonous routine
■ May have to stand or walk for extended periods

POPULATION GROUPS
■ Part-Time/Temporary
■ Job Complement
■ Senior Citizen
■ General

PREPARATION
■ No formal education is required
■ Military or law enforcement background is helpful
■ Most employers prefer at least a high school diploma
■ May have to undergo a background check and a drug test
■ Almost every state has licensing or registration requirements for security guards who work for contract security agencies. To be granted a license, you generally must be 18 years of age, have no convictions for perjury or acts of violence, pass a background investigation, and complete classroom training on a variety of subjects, including property rights, emergency procedures, and capture of suspected criminals.

CERTIFICATION
■ Certification is not usually associated with this occupation

RELATED JOBS/TITLES
■ Bodyguard
■ Police Officer
■ Private Detective
■ Investigator
■ Corrections Officer

EARNINGS

■ $12,860 to $17,570 to $28,660

OUTLOOK

■ According to the *Occupational Outlook Handbook*, jobs for security guards are projected to grow faster than the average through 2010. Many job openings will be created as a result of the high turnover of workers in this field.

FOR MORE INFORMATION

For information on industrial security, contact:

American Society for Industrial Security
1625 Prince Street
Alexandria, VA 22314-2818
703-519-6200
asis@asisonline.org
http://www.asisonline.org

For information on union membership, contact:

International Union, Security, Police, and Fire Professionals of America
25510 Kelly Road
Roseville, MI 40866
800-228-7492
http://www.spfpa.org

■ Shipping and Receiving Clerk

A shipping and receiving clerk maintains records of materials shipped and received. Duties may include preparing shipments; accepting deliveries; assembling, stamping, verifying, and preparing documents; attaching and checking address mailing labels; checking condition of merchandise; checking for possible errors; filling orders; wrapping or packing; computing postal rates; preparing invoices; relaying information to other offices; moving and lifting merchandise; computer data entry; and arranging for proper department delivery.

MAY BE GOOD FOR YOU NOW IF YOU

- Want to work part-time
- Like physical work
- Have prior experience in shipping or as a mailroom clerk
- Enjoy details and numbers
- Have basic math skills
- Are computer-proficient

HELPFUL PERSONAL TRAITS

- Good communication skills
- Good health and physical stamina
- Manual dexterity
- Good vision
- Detail-oriented

VALUE TO YOUR CAREER DEVELOPMENT

- May help meet the values of achievement, skill, and serving others
- Satisfaction derived from knowing that a shipment sent out or received has been expedited efficiently

VALUE TO EMPLOYER/SOCIETY

- Saves employer significant cost if well done
- Helps ensure that customers receive valued items without delay or damage
- Contributes to the effective movement of millions of packages each year, which is vital to the economic health of the country

POSSIBLE DOWNSIDES
- May have to work in cool environment or outdoors in poor weather
- Requires bending, standing, lifting, walking, and reaching
- May be stressful during rush periods or busy seasons
- May have to ship or receive hazardous materials

POPULATION GROUPS
- Part-Time/Temporary
- General

PREPARATION
- High school diploma
- On-the-job training is provided by the employer
- Computer skills are helpful

CERTIFICATION
- Certification is not usually associated with this occupation

RELATED JOBS/TITLES
- Shipping Clerk
- Receiving Clerk
- Stock Clerk
- Cargo/Freight Agent
- Traffic Clerk

EARNINGS
- $14,750 to $21,880 to $34,370

OUTLOOK
- According to the *Occupational Outlook Handbook,* jobs for shipping and receiving clerks are projected to grow more slowly than the average through 2010. Large and medium-sized companies are increasingly using computers to store and retrieve records. Computerized conveyor systems, robotics, and trucks, as well as scanners are increasing productivity and eliminating the need for large numbers of workers.

FOR MORE INFORMATION
For more information, contact:

American Society of Transportation and Logistics
5100 Poplar Avenue, Suite 522
Memphis, TN 38137
901-415-6800
http://www.astl.org

National Retail Federation
325 7th Street, NW, Suite 1100
Washington, DC 20004-2802
202-783-7971
http://www.nrf.com

■ Social Service Assistant

Social service assistants perform a wide variety of social help tasks, usually under the direction of one or more professionals. Tasks vary depending on which field the worker works in, such as social work, psychology, psychiatry, rehabilitation, or nursing, for example. Some common duties include helping people correctly complete paperwork for obtaining benefits and services; determining eligibility for food stamps; assisting with insurance forms; arranging for transportation or escort service; helping to resolve tenant-landlord conflicts; keeping records; monitoring client progress and submitting reports to supervisors; providing emotional support; and transporting and/or accompanying clients to and from meal sites, adult day care, doctor's offices, and other appointments.

MAY BE GOOD FOR YOU NOW IF YOU
- Desire job experience that will eventually lead to a profession in social work
- Like direct contact with people who need help with social, emotional, and mental problems
- Need volunteer experience in this area

HELPFUL PERSONAL TRAITS
- Kind, sensitive, and patient
- Responsible
- Good at responding quickly and maintaining composure in stressful situations
- Work well with people of all backgrounds and ages
- Good at observing, evaluating, and solving problems

VALUE TO YOUR CAREER DEVELOPMENT
- Can help meet the values of helping others, love, health, and emotional well-being
- Satisfaction derived from helping minimize or alleviate some of the struggles many have in our society

VALUE TO EMPLOYER/SOCIETY
- Helps to meet a continuing need in American society
- Enables social work professionals to do their jobs more effectively

- Helps to lessen the chances for more serious health problems, crime, and family conflicts

POSSIBLE DOWNSIDES
- Low pay
- Can be tiring mentally and emotionally
- May have to work in understaffed situation with a heavy workload

POPULATION GROUPS
- Single Parent
- Senior Citizen
- Volunteer
- General

PREPARATION
- Although a high school diploma is usually not required, certification or associate's degree credentials are increasingly preferred
- May be required to have background checks and drug tests

CERTIFICATION
- Certificate and associate's degree programs in human services or mental health are offered at community and junior colleges, vocational-technical institutes, and other postsecondary institutions. Programs typically include courses in psychology, sociology, crisis intervention, family dynamics, therapeutic interviewing, rehabilitation, and gerontology.

RELATED JOBS/TITLES
- Case Management Aide
- Human Resource Aide
- Human Service Aide
- Adult Day Care Worker
- Home Care Aide
- Gerontology Aide
- Community Outreach Worker

- Physical Therapist Aide
- Occupational Therapist Aide

EARNINGS

- $14,660 to $22,330 to $35,220

OUTLOOK

- According to the *Occupational Outlook Handbook,* jobs for social service aides are expected to be among the fastest growing job areas through 2010. The best opportunities will be in job-training programs, residential care facilities, and private social service agencies, which include such services as adult day care and meal delivery programs. Correctional facilities are also expected to employ many more human services workers.

FOR MORE INFORMATION

For more information on careers in counseling, contact:

American Counseling Association
5999 Stevenson Avenue
Alexandria, VA 22304-3300
800-347-6647
http://www.counseling.org

For information on employment with government human service agencies, contact:

The U.S. Department of Health and Human Services
200 Independence Avenue, SW
Washington, DC 20201
202-619-0257
http://www.hhs.gov

For information on student memberships, scholarships, and the online career pamphlet, The Human Services Worker, *check the following Web site:*

National Organization for Human Service Education
University of Rhode Island
107 Quinn Hall, URI
Kingston, RI 02881
http://www.nohse.com

■ Stock Clerk

A stock clerk receives, unpacks, and stocks and replenishes shelves, counters, and other areas with merchandise in either wholesale or retail establishments. Responsibilities include unpacking, checking, counting, sorting, and tracking merchandise or supplies. Stock clerks also keep records of what is received or taken out of stock, inspect damaged goods, and organize and mark items with prices and inventory-control codes. They may also be required to lift and transport merchandise to sales areas or warehouses. Tools and equipment used include computers, calculators, scanners, pricing guns, forklifts, box openers, and pliers.

MAY BE GOOD FOR YOU NOW IF YOU
- Don't mind doing hard work
- Have worked in stockrooms or mailrooms before
- Want to work part-time
- Need to supplement income or earn money for school
- Have customer service skills
- Have computer skills
- Have math, reading, and writing proficiency

HELPFUL PERSONAL TRAITS
- Physically strong
- Stamina
- Responsible and alert
- Good health, vision, and manual dexterity
- Honest

VALUE TO YOUR CAREER DEVELOPMENT
- Can help meet values of achievement, skill, variety, knowledge, and serving others
- Satisfaction derived from completing a stocking assignment effectively, maintaining order, and organizing inventory

VALUE TO EMPLOYER/SOCIETY
- Part of a team that helps work flow, satisfies customer demands, and speeds order fulfillment

- Placing items in appropriate areas where they can be easily seen and retrieved encourages customers to buy, and positively affects revenues

POSSIBLE DOWNSIDES

- Must do a lot of lifting, bending, reaching, and standing
- Increased risk of falls and back strain
- May experience stress from dealing with back orders, late arrivals, and deadline pressures
- May be monotonous and boring

POPULATION GROUPS

- Part-Time/Temporary
- General

PREPARATION

- No high school diploma is required
- Employer provides on-the-job training
- Computer and math skills are helpful

CERTIFICATION

- Certification is not usually associated with this occupation

RELATED JOBS/TITLES

- Inventory Clerk
- Stock Control Clerk
- Warehouse Worker
- Shipping Clerk
- Cargo/Freight Clerk

EARNINGS

- $12,720 to $18,210 to $33,970

OUTLOOK

- According to the *Occupational Outlook Handbook,* jobs for stock clerks are projected to grow more slowly than the average through 2010. This is a result of increased automation and other productivity improvements that enable clerks to handle more stock. Because this occupation employs a large number of workers, many job openings will occur each year to replace stock clerks who transfer to other jobs. Stock clerk jobs tend to be entry-level positions, so many vacancies will be created by normal career progression to other occupations.

FOR MORE INFORMATION

For materials on educational programs in the retail industry, contact:

National Retail Federation
325 7th Street, NW, Suite 1100
Washington, DC 20004
202-783-7971
http://www.nrf.com

■ Teacher Aide

A teacher aide provides instructional and clerical assistance for teachers. Responsibilities vary but can include tutoring; supervising students during recess, lunchtime, and on field trips; recording grades; monitoring individualized lessons; preparing materials and equipment; and overseeing various activities assigned by the instructor. Other duties may include helping students in small groups, reviewing lessons to prepare students for tests, and setting up exhibits.

MAY BE GOOD FOR YOU NOW IF YOU
■ Desire to work part-time

■ Want to work with students

■ Want to volunteer

■ Plan to become a teacher or have a career in education

HELPFUL PERSONAL TRAITS
■ Good communication skills

■ Patient

■ Kind, but firm

■ Friendly

■ Detail-oriented

■ Persuasive

■ Good listener

VALUE TO YOUR CAREER DEVELOPMENT
■ Can help meet values of education, helping others, achievement, recognition, and knowledge

■ Satisfaction derived from helping others learn and succeed

VALUE TO EMPLOYER/SOCIETY
■ Helps to meet the critical need in many schools for paraprofessional assistance

■ Provides relief to regular teachers, which can improve their emotional well-being and enable them to better meet the educational needs of students

POSSIBLE DOWNSIDES
- Low pay
- Can be emotionally, physically, and mentally fatiguing
- May be monotonous at times
- Could involve some lifting

POPULATION GROUPS
- Part-Time/Temporary
- Limited Disabled
- Single Parent
- Senior Citizen
- General

PREPARATION
- In school districts where aides perform mostly clerical duties, a high school diploma or GED is the minimum requirement. Teacher aides who work in the classroom may be required to take some college courses and attend in-service training and special teacher conferences and seminars.
- Specific job skills are learned on the job
- Experience working with children is helpful

CERTIFICATION
- Certification is not usually associated with this occupation However, some community and junior colleges have certificate and associate's degree programs that prepare teacher aides for classroom work, offering courses in child development, health and safety, and child guidance.

RELATED JOBS/TITLES
- Teacher Assistant
- Teacher
- Library Assistant
- Child Care Worker
- Occupational Therapist Assistant

EARNINGS
- $12,260 to $17,350 to $27,550

OUTLOOK

■ According to the *Occupational Outlook Handbook,* jobs for teacher aides are projected to grow faster than average through 2010. A shortage of teachers will motivate administrators to hire more aides to help with larger classrooms. Because of increased responsibilities for aides, state departments of education will likely establish standards of training. The National Resource Center for Paraprofessionals in Education and Related Services is designing national standards for paraeducator training. Jobs should be especially easy to find in special education, day care, and extended-day programs.

FOR MORE INFORMATION

To learn about current issues affecting paraprofessionals in education, visit the AFT Web site or contact:

American Federation of Teachers (AFT)
555 New Jersey Avenue, NW
Washington, DC 20001
202-879-4400
online@aft.org
http://www.aft.org

To order publications or read current research and other information, contact:

Association for Childhood Education International
17904 Georgia Avenue, Suite 215
Olney, MD 20832
301-570-2111
http://www.udel.edu/bateman/acei

For information about training programs and other resources, contact:

National Resource Center for Paraprofessionals
Utah State University
6526 Old Main Hill
Logan, UT 84322-6526
435-797-7272
http://www.nrcpara.org

■ Travel Agent

A travel agent assists tourists and travelers by giving advice about places to visit and making arrangements for transportation, hotel accommodations, car rentals, tours, and recreational site visits. Other tasks may include promoting travel packages; assessing travelers' needs; and providing information about passport and visa regulations, foreign currency and exchange, climate and wardrobe, health requirements, customs regulations, baggage and accident insurance, traveler's checks or letters of credit, car rentals, tourist attractions, and welcome or escort services. Travel agents use computers to compare travel-related information, such as air transportation departure and arrival times, air fares, and hotel ratings and accommodations. They sometimes visit some of the travel sites they recommend to customers to rate their comfort, cleanliness, and quality of service.

MAY BE GOOD FOR YOU NOW IF YOU
■ Want to be self-employed or work from home
■ Love traveling and want to become a tour guide or own a travel agency in the future
■ Are retired, have traveled extensively, and want to earn extra income

HELPFUL PERSONAL TRAITS
■ Good listener and observant
■ Patient
■ Good communication skills
■ Strong computer and writing skills
■ Friendly
■ Detail-oriented
■ Good at solving problems
■ Organized
■ Persuasive
■ Knowledgeable

VALUE TO YOUR CAREER DEVELOPMENT
■ Can help meet values of travel, helping others, and knowledge

Short-Term Job Training: 50 Good Jobs   163

■ Satisfaction derived from helping others in their pursuit of recreation and pleasure

VALUE TO EMPLOYER/SOCIETY
■ Helps arrange safe, efficient, cost-effective travel for millions of business and pleasure travelers

POSSIBLE DOWNSIDES
■ May have to work long hours

■ May be pressured to provide an array of services in a short time period

■ Job outlook especially sensitive to economic fluctuations

POPULATION GROUPS
■ Part-Time/Temporary

■ Senior Citizen

■ Volunteer

■ General

PREPARATION
■ Can usually enter with a high school diploma but some specialized training or experience beyond high school is helpful

■ On-the-job training is normally provided by travel agencies

■ Travel experience and computer skills are advantages

CERTIFICATION
■ To be able to sell passage on various types of transportation, a travel agent must be approved by the conferences of carriers involved. These are the Airlines Reporting Corporation, the International Air Transport Association, Cruise Lines International Association, and the Rail Travel Promotion Agency. To sell tickets for these individual conferences, the agent must be clearly established in the travel business and have a good personal and business background. Not all travel agents are authorized to sell passage by all of the above conferences. Naturally, those who wish to sell the widest range of services should seek affiliation with all four.

Currently, travel agents are not required to be federally licensed. The following states require some form of registration or licensing: California, Florida, Hawaii, Illinois, Iowa, Ohio, Oregon, Rhode Island, and Washington.

The Institute of Certified Travel Agents (ICTA) offers voluntary certification as Certified Travel Associate (CTA) and Certified Travel Counselor (CTC). ICTA also offers travel agents a number of other programs such as sales skills development courses and destination specialist courses, which provide a detailed knowledge of various geographic regions of the world.

RELATED JOBS/TITLES
■ Travel Consultant
■ Travel Specialist
■ Tourist Information Officer
■ Reservation Clerk
■ Tour Guide

EARNINGS
■ $15,900 to $25,150 to $39,300

OUTLOOK
■ According to the *Occupational Outlook Handbook,* jobs for travel agents are projected to grow more slowly than the average through 2010. Future prospects in the travel industry will depend to some degree on the state of the economy and the perceived level of travel safety in the wake of the terrorist attacks of September 2001. Most airlines and other travel suppliers now offer consumers the option of making their own travel arrangements through online reservation services. With this as an option, travelers are becoming less dependent upon agents to make travel arrangements. However, the travel industry is expected to continue to expand as more Americans travel for pleasure and business.

FOR MORE INFORMATION

Visit the ASTA Web site to read the online pamphlet, Becoming a Travel Agent.

American Society of Travel Agents (ASTA)
1101 King Street, Suite 200
Alexandria, VA 22314
703-739-2782
askasta@astahq.com
http://www.astanet.com

For information regarding the travel industry and certification, contact:

Institute of Certified Travel Agents
148 Linden Street
PO Box 812059
Wellesley, MA 02482
800-542-4282
http://www.icta.com

For information on travel careers in the U.S. government, contact:

Society of Government Travel Professionals
6935 Wisconsin Avenue, Suite 200
Bethesda, MD 20815
301-654-8595
govtvlmkt@aol.com
http://www.government-travel.org

For general information on the travel industry, contact:

Travel Industry Association of America
1100 New York Avenue, NW, Suite 450
Washington, DC 20005-3934
202-408-8422
http://www.tia.org

■ Truck Driver

Truck drivers drive trucks to and from particular destinations usually for the purpose of delivering or picking-up goods of all types, sizes, weights, and shapes. Other job duties may include conducting safety checks, performing fuel and oil checks, loading and unloading cargo, arranging goods on the truck, securing cargo, acquiring confirmation signatures, maintaining and submitting records, and communicating and working with dispatchers. Some truck drivers may be short-haul (local) drivers, while others are long-distance (intercity or interstate) drivers and may have another driver to assist.

MAY BE GOOD FOR YOU NOW IF YOU
■ Like the adventure of driving and experiencing new places
■ Don't mind working and traveling at night or on weekends
■ Prefer to work alone
■ Want an entry-level experience in the trucking industry

HELPFUL PERSONAL TRAITS
■ Independent worker
■ Dependable
■ Observant
■ Good health and eyesight
■ Good eye-hand coordination
■ Good communication skills

VALUE TO YOUR CAREER DEVELOPMENT
■ Can help meet the values of power, achievement, adventure, and helping others
■ Satisfaction derived from successfully completing trips on time

VALUE TO EMPLOYER/SOCIETY
■ Transports vital goods necessary for the economic survival of companies across America
■ Truckers provide a valuable service in the shipping industry by transporting goods that cannot be shipped by air or water

POSSIBLE DOWNSIDES

- May be fatiguing
- Long-distance drivers may spend a lot of time away from home and family
- May suffer boredom and loneliness
- May have to drive in poor weather

POPULATION GROUPS

- Part-Time/Temporary
- General

PREPARATION

- Training varies widely from on-the-job, ride-along training to employer-sponsored classes that last from a few days to several weeks
- Completion of a driver-training program certified by the Professional Truck Driver Institute of America is an advantage.
- Must have a valid driver's license or commercial driver's license (CDL)
- Age requirements vary from 18 to 21 years (you must be 21 years old to qualify for interstate trucking)
- Must meet minimum vision and physical requirements as well as any state/federal guidelines
- May be asked to take a drug test

CERTIFICATION

- The Professional Truck Institute of America provides a free list of certified tractor-trailer driver training programs

RELATED JOBS/TITLES

- Bus Driver
- Ambulance Driver
- Taxi Driver
- Chauffeur

EARNINGS

- $20,000 to $40,000 to $52,000

OUTLOOK

■ According to the *Occupational Outlook Handbook*, jobs for truck drivers are projected to increase about as fast as the average through 2010. Employment of heavy and tractor-trailer truck drivers is expected to grow by 23.3 percent between 2000 and 2010, according to the U.S. Department of Labor. Employment of light and delivery truck drivers is expected to grow by 13.7 percent in the same period. Currently, there is a shortage of both local and over-the-road drivers.

FOR MORE INFORMATION

For further information and literature about a career as a truck driver, contact the following organizations:

American Trucking Associations
2200 Mill Road
Alexandria, VA 22314-4677
703-838-1700
http://www.trucking.org

Professional Truck Driver Institute
2200 Mill Road
Alexandria, VA 22314
703-838-8842
http://www.ptdi.org

■ Vending Machine Servicer/Repairer

A vending machine servicer/repairer is a worker who installs, services, and stocks vending and amusement machines. Duties may include collecting money from machines, restocking, updating labels, cleaning and repairing, preventive maintenance, installation and replacement of machines and parts, lubricating, conducting diagnostic testing, and adjusting coin changers. Other tasks include keeping records, preparing cost estimates, and ordering parts.

MAY BE GOOD FOR YOU NOW IF YOU

■ Are good with your hands and like tinkering with mechanical things

■ Have worked as a mechanic before

■ Have some experience or training in electronics

HELPFUL PERSONAL TRAITS

■ Mechanically inclined

■ Good at reading and understanding technical/service manuals and diagrams

■ Trustworthy

■ Manual dexterity

■ Independent

VALUE TO YOUR CAREER DEVELOPMENT

■ May help meet the values of achievement, skill, and helping others

■ Satisfaction derived from repairing a machine and restoring service

VALUE TO EMPLOYER/SOCIETY

■ Working vending machines are important in places where there are limited opportunities to obtain meals

■ Helps to provide lunch, snacks, and beverages for people who work in or visit businesses, factories, hotels, retail establishments, schools, and other locations

POSSIBLE DOWNSIDES
▪ At risk for electrical shock

▪ May have to move heavy machines and transport heavy cargo

POPULATION GROUPS
▪ Single Parent

▪ Part-Time/Temporary

▪ Limited Disabled

PREPARATION
▪ A high school diploma is preferred

▪ On-the-job training is usually provided by employers

▪ Background in electrical work, refrigeration, and machine repair is an advantage

▪ Must have a valid driver's license and a good driving record

CERTIFICATION
▪ Certification is not usually associated with this occupation

RELATED JOBS/TITLES
▪ Electrical/Electronics Installer and Repairer

▪ Heating, Air-Conditioning, and Refrigeration Mechanic

▪ Home Appliance Repairer

EARNINGS
▪ $14,690 to $25,660 to $40,570

OUTLOOK
▪ According to the *Occupational Outlook Handbook,* jobs for vending machine servicer/repairers are projected to grow about as fast as the average through 2010. Opportunities should be good for workers with some knowledge of electronics. Additional vending machines are likely to be installed in industrial plants, hospitals, stores, and schools to meet the public demand for inexpensive snacks and other food items. Also, there is an increased need for vending machines in businesses with few employees.

Vending machines will become more automated and dispense a wider range of products. They will begin to incorporate microwave ovens, mini refrigerators, and freezers.

FOR MORE INFORMATION

For general information on vending machine repair, contact:

Automatic Merchandiser Vending Group
Cygnus Business Media
PO Box 803
1233 Junesville Avenue
Fort Atkinson, WI 53538-0803

For information on the vending industry and access to a job bank, contact:

National Automatic Merchandising Association
20 North Wacker Drive, Suite 3500
Chicago, IL 60606
http://www.vending.org

■ Welder

A welder joins together metal parts by applying heat and sometimes pressure until they melt and form a permanent bond. Duties include soldering, brazing, reading and interpreting schematic drawings or blueprints, selecting and setting up equipment, examining welds, loading parts, operating welding equipment, and adhering to safety procedures. Welders work on constructing and repairing automobiles, aircraft, ships, buildings, bridges, highways, appliances, and many other metal structures and manufactured products. They may travel to construction sites, utility installations, and other locations to make on-site repairs to metalwork.

MAY BE GOOD FOR YOU NOW IF YOU
■ Have taken and enjoyed welding classes
■ Are able to work in awkward positions
■ Enjoy making things with your hands

HELPFUL PERSONAL TRAITS
■ Good physical condition and 20/20 vision
■ Patient
■ Good eye-hand coordination
■ Accurate and detail-oriented
■ Manual dexterity
■ Safety-conscious

VALUE TO YOUR CAREER DEVELOPMENT
■ May help meet the values of skill, variety, and knowledge
■ Satisfaction derived from having made something and completed a project according to specifications

VALUE TO EMPLOYER/SOCIETY
■ Makes it possible for others to perform their jobs
■ Contributes to the construction and repair of vehicles, buildings, bridges, appliances, and other metal structures and products

POSSIBLE DOWNSIDES
- Exposure to dangers of eye damage, fumes, and burns
- May have to work long hours
- May have to work in poor weather
- Bending, crouching, and working in awkward positions may be required

POPULATION GROUPS
- General

PREPARATION
- Varies from a few weeks of on-the-job training to several years of combined school and work training
- Community colleges, technical institutes, trade schools, and the armed forces offer formal training programs in welding
- Computer proficiency may be helpful

CERTIFICATION
- To do welding work where the strength of the weld is a critical factor (such as in aircraft, bridges, boilers, or high-pressure pipelines), welders may have to pass employer tests or standardized examinations for certification by government agencies or professional and technical associations. The American Welding Society offers the Certified Welder (CW) and Certified Welding Fabricator (CWF) certifications.

RELATED JOBS/TITLES
- Solderer
- Brazier
- Cutter
- Machine Operator

EARNINGS
- $18,430 to $27,300 to $43,140

OUTLOOK
- According to the *Occupational Outlook Handbook,* jobs for welders are projected to grow about as fast as the average through 2010. There should be plenty of opportunities for

skilled welders, since many employers have difficulties in finding qualified applicants.

FOR MORE INFORMATION
For information on education and certification, contact:

American Welding Society
550 LeJeune Road, NW
Miami, FL 33126
800-443-9353
http://www.aws.org

For more information about becoming a welder, contact:

International Association of Machinists and Aerospace Workers
9000 Machinists Place
Upper Marlboro, MD 20772-2687
301-967-4500
http://www.iamaw.org

■ Water/Liquid Waste Treatment Plant Operator

A water/liquid waste treatment plant operator oversees processes that treat water to remove dangerous pollutants caused by domestic and industrial liquid waste and distribute treated water to customers and the environment. Some day-to-day duties include reading, interpreting, and adjusting meters and gauges; operating chemical-releasing devices; securing water samples; conducting lab analyses; and doing minor repairs on valves, pumps, and other equipment. Other tasks include implementing emergency response techniques and staying abreast of federal, state, and municipal guidelines and regulations. Water/liquid waste treatment plant operators must use computers and safety equipment.

MAY BE GOOD FOR YOU NOW IF YOU
■ Desire to work in the environmental-protection field
■ Like challenges

HELPFUL PERSONAL TRAITS
■ Observant and alert
■ Mechanical aptitude
■ Manual dexterity
■ Able to keep composure under stressful conditions
■ Responsible
■ Conscientious

VALUE TO YOUR CAREER DEVELOPMENT
■ Can help meet the values of health, safety, helping others, and knowledge
■ Satisfaction derived from knowing you are doing important work to conserve and protect natural resources

VALUE TO EMPLOYER/SOCIETY
■ Crucial to public health and safety
■ Helps ensure a safe water supply and prevention of sickness or disease that might be caused by harmful pollutants in water, soil, and vegetation

POSSIBLE DOWNSIDES
▪ May experience high stress and danger during times of emergency
▪ Noisy and sometimes unclean

POPULATION GROUPS
▪ General

PREPARATION
▪ High school diploma usually preferred
▪ Basic math, biology, chemistry, and mechanical background are recommended
▪ Must pass a written exam as well as a certification exam in most states
▪ Specialized education in wastewater technology is available in two-year programs that lead to an associate's degree and one-year programs that lead to a certificate. These programs are offered at some community and junior colleges and vocational-technical institutes.

CERTIFICATION
▪ Workers who control operations at wastewater treatment plants must be certified in most states. Many states issue several classes of certification, depending on the size of the plant the worker is qualified to control. Certification may be beneficial even if it is not a requirement and may make workers eligible for higher pay.

RELATED JOBS/TITLES
▪ Waste Water Treatment Plant and Systems Operator
▪ Power Plant Operator
▪ Gas Plant Operator
▪ Chemical Plant Operator
▪ Refinery Operator

EARNINGS
▪ $19,120 to $31,380 to $47,370

OUTLOOK
▪ According to the *Occupational Outlook Handbook,* jobs for water/liquid waste treatment plant operators are projected to

grow as fast as the average through 2010. Workers in wastewater treatment plants are rarely laid off, even during a recession, because wastewater treatment is essential to public health and welfare. In the future, more wastewater professionals will probably be employed by private companies that contract to manage treatment plants for local governments. Operators and technicians with formal training will have the best chances for new positions and promotions.

FOR MORE INFORMATION

For information on environmental certifications, contact:

Association of Boards of Certification
208 Fifth Street
Ames, IA 50010-6259
http://www.abccert.org

For information on the water quality industry, career opportunities, and workshops, contact:

Water Environment Federation
601 Wythe Street
Alexandria, VA 22314-1994
http://www.wef.org

For current information on the field of wastewater management, contact:

American Water Works Association
6666 West Quincy Avenue
Denver, CO 80235
303-794-7711
http://www.awwa.org

For information on education and training, contact:

Environmental Careers Organization
179 South Street
Boston, MA 02111
617-426-4375
http://www.eco.org

National Environmental Training Association
5320 North 16th Street, Suite 114
Phoenix, AZ 85016
602-956-6099
neta@ehs-training.org
http://www.ehs-training.org

For career information, contact or visit the following Web site:

Water Environment Federation
601 Wythe Street
Alexandria, VA 22314-1994
800-666-0206
http://www.wef.org

CHAPTER THREE

CERTIFICATION JOB OPTIONS

Certification has not received much attention until the last few years. Today's proliferation of certification programs can be attributed, in part, to the phenomenal growth of technology and availability of information. This rapid growth has rendered traditional means of acquiring training (college degrees and apprenticeships) slow and inadequate for meeting the huge demand for a workforce that is abreast of and skilled in the new technologies. Certification programs, many of which can be completed in one year or less (although some require a much longer period of time), have filled the gap.

Certification is an attractive option for both employers and employees. Employers whose businesses depend on technology are showing more respect for certification with increased financial compensation and benefits. Certified individuals receive recognition and greater job satisfaction without having to spend several years and significant amounts of money in preparation. A number of other reasons for the popularity of certification programs were summarized in an article by Sandy Kerka in the Winter 2001 edition of *Career Development.* (See Bibliography of Print and Web Resources, p. 293.) According to Kerka, certificate programs can serve as an introduction for adult students leery about making a more formal degree commitment; they can provide people who already hold degrees with high-need skills in a short time; and they can enhance current training.

Some of the additional benefits of certification are:

1. Provides status within an industry that recognizes you are certified and have acquired a minimum level of knowledge and skill

2. Gives you recognition by fellow workers and supervisors that you have developed a level of expertise in a valued area

3. Instills confidence in consumers that you are qualified to efficiently provide a service, deliver a product, or complete a task

4. Increases your opportunities for advancement and higher wages

5. Increases your choices for career opportunities and employers

6. Increases your marketability and competitive edge

7. Gives you a greater sense of job achievement and self-esteem

8. Provides more alternatives for laid-off or retired workers who need retraining and upgrading of current skills

9. Helps enhance the reputation of your employer who can claim a qualified, certified staff

10. Provides a quantifiable indicator of a certain level of work quality that can be expected

11. Serves as preparation for, or may improve your chances for, acceptance into a graduate-level program

While the widespread popularity and growth seems to be relatively recent, certification itself is not new. In the computer and health industries, certification has been quite common for some time and may explain why these two occupational areas are leaders in the promotion of certification. However, even in these two industries certification has been fragmented. In the past, certification granters had obvious vested interests; for example, product manufacturers offered certification in the use of their own products, or developers of training programs offered their certification attached to the completion of their own courses. Although this still occurs today, certification efforts are becoming more standardized and objective and are increasingly accepted and sponsored by professional associations. Many of these organizations are taking the responsibility for developing common standards for certification proficiencies that will be accepted by most within the industry they represent. Such standardization can provide transferability to different companies and different locations and possibly open the door for more college-credit-equivalency acceptance.

While standard acceptance of certification is occurring in more industries, there are still cautions to take when evaluating certification programs. Here is a short list of questions to ask if you are seriously considering a certificate program:

■ Is the certification recognized only by your current employer?

■ Who are the other employers that recognize your certification?

- Has the premier association in your occupational area endorsed and accepted the certification?

- Will the quality and credibility of the certificate be valid for only a short period of time?

- Is your certification in an area that is likely to be in demand for a long time?

- What is the track record of others who hold this certification?

- Is the certification offered by colleges and universities? Which ones? What is the cost? How much time it will take?

- Can you receive equivalent or better training at a local community or technical college?

Certification Programs Offered by Private Companies, Vendors, Nonprofit Organizations, and Similar Institutions

Please note that this is just a sampling of certification programs. It is by no means an exhaustive list, but it should provide a starting place for your own research. You should also check the For More Information section at the end of each career profile in this chapter.

INFORMATION TECHNOLOGY

The information technology (IT) industry appears to be the front-runner in terms of certification. According to an article published in the *Technical Education Research Monitor* (*TERM*), the IT industry awarded a minimum of 1.7 million certificates worldwide in 1999. (See Bibliography of Print and Web Resources, p. 293.) The certifications listed represent just a few that are available. The IT industry undergoes constant change, and new certifications are frequently added. Check with the sponsoring companies or institutions for further information. It is also recommended that you research other software and hardware manufacturers and IT organizations.

Cisco
http://www.cisco.com/warp/public/10/wwtraining/
Cisco Certified Network Associate (CCNA)
Cisco Certified Network Professional (CCNP)
Cisco Certified Design Associate (CCDA)
Cisco Certified Design Professional (CCDP)

COMPUTER TECHNOLOGY INDUSTRY ASSOCIATION
http://www.comptia.org
A+

INSTITUTE FOR CERTIFICATION OF COMPUTING PROFESSIONALS
http://www.iccp.org
Certified Computing Professional (CCP)

MICROSOFT
http://www.microsoft.com/traincert/default.asp
Microsoft Certified Professional (MCP)
Microsoft Certified Systems Engineer (MCSE)
Microsoft Certified Solution Developer (MCSD)
Microsoft Certified Professional + Internet (MCP+I)
Microsoft Certified Professional + Site Building (MCP+SB)

NOVELL
http://www.novell.com/education/certinfo/
Certified Novell Administrator (CAN)
Certified Novell Engineer (CNE)

ORACLE
http://www.oracle.com/education/certification/
Oracle Certified Professional Database Operator (OCP DBO)
Oracle Certified Professional Application Developer (OCP AD)
Oracle Certified Professional Database Administrator (OCP
    DBA)
Oracle Certified Professional Java Developer (OCP Java Dev.)

HEALTH CARE
Listed below are several certification programs related to the
health industry, another field that has been a leader in the certification movement.

AMERICAN CERTIFIED NURSE-MIDWIFE CERTIFICATION COUNCIL
http://www.accmidwife.org
Certified Nurse-Midwife (CNM)

COUNCIL ON CERTIFICATION OF NURSE ANESTHETISTS
http://www.catinc.com/clients/ccna.htm
Certified Registered Nurse Anesthetist

NATIONAL BOARD FOR RESPIRATORY CARE
http://www.nbrc.org
Certified Respiratory Therapist (CRT)

NATIONAL CREDENTIALING AGENCY FOR LABORATORY
PERSONNEL
http://www.nca-info.org
Medical Laboratory Technician (MLT)

NATIONAL STRENGTH PROFESSIONALS ASSOCIATION
http://www.nspainc.com
Certified Personal Trainer (CPT)
Certified Functional Exercise Specialist (CFES)
Certified Conditioning Specialist (CCS)
Post-Rehab Certification

PHARMACY TECHNICIAN CERTIFICATION BOARD
http://www.ptcb.org
Certified Pharmacy Technician (CPhT)

OTHER CERTIFICATIONS
ASSOCIATED BUILDERS AND CONTRACTORS
http://www.abc.org
Construction Education Professional (CEP)

THE CAREER PLANNING AND ADULT DEVELOPMENT NETWORK
http://www.careernetwork.org/career_workshops.html
Job and Career Transition Coach (JCTC)

NATIONAL ASSOCIATION OF HOME BUILDERS
http://www.nahb.com/consumers/remodeling/cgr.htm
Certified Graduate Remodeler (CGR)
Certified Aging-in-Place Specialist (CAPS)

JUNIOR, COMMUNITY, AND TECHNICAL COLLEGES
Certification programs are nothing new for most junior, community, and technical colleges in America. They are an important part of the educational offerings at these institutions in their effort to meet the just-in-time needs of employers in nearby communities. Some college certificate programs award college credit that can be applied toward an associate's or bachelor's degree. Other offerings are non-college-credit vocational certificate programs. Vocational certificate programs are often designed to meet the

needs of local employees who need to upgrade current skills or want to advance.

AUSTIN COMMUNITY COLLEGE
AUSTIN, TEXAS
http://www.austin.cc.tx.us
Diagnostic Medical Sonography
Human Services
Motorcycle Repair
Interpreter Preparation Program
International Business
Medical Coding Specialist

J. SARGEANT REYNOLDS COMMUNITY COLLEGE
RICHMOND, VIRGINIA
http://www.jsr.cc.va.us
Automotive Technology
Dental Assisting
Fire Science Technology
Music Recording Technology

MIAMI-DADE COMMUNITY COLLEGE
MIAMI, FLORIDA
http://www3.mdcc.edu
Embalming
Airline Reservation and Ticketing Agent
Air Cargo Agent
Bail Bonding
Correctional Officer

SACRAMENTO CITY COLLEGE
SACRAMENTO, CALIFORNIA
http://www.scc.losrios.edu
Private Security Services
Surveying
Electrical Power Lighting Systems
Gerontology
Publications Specialist

YORK COUNTY TECHNICAL COLLEGE
WELLS, MAINE
http://www.yctc.net
Cisco Networking Specialist
Early Childhood Education
Lodging Operation
Small Business Management

BACHELOR'S DEGREE INSTITUTIONS

Certification programs are increasingly being offered at bachelor's-degree-granting colleges and universities. A growing number of programs in high-need employment areas are now available at the bachelor's, post-bachelor's and post-master's degree levels. The required time to complete both certification and vocational certificate programs vary greatly, from two days to a few weeks to several months.

ASSUMPTION COLLEGE
WORCESTER, MASSACHUSETTS
http://www.assumption.edu
Certificate of Professional Studies (CPS) (post-MBA)
Certificate of Advanced Graduate Studies (CAGS)

DEPAUL UNIVERSITY
CHICAGO, ILLINOIS
http://www.depaul.edu
Certificate Program in Financial Planning
Fundamentals of Human Resources Program
Post-Master's Certification Program

JOHNS HOPKINS UNIVERSITY
BALTIMORE, MARYLAND
http://www.jhu.edu
Graduate Certificate Program in Public Health (GCP)

OREGON STATE UNIVERSITY
CORVALLIS, OREGON
http://www.orst.edu
Gerontology Certificate (post-bachelor's)
Certificate of Applied Ethics

UNIVERSITY OF FLORIDA
GAINESVILLE, FLORIDA
http://www.ufl.edu
Decisions and Information Science Certificate (master's level)
Certificate in Biomedical Engineering (master's level)
Electronic Countermeasures Test and Evaluation Certificate

UNIVERSITY OF LOUISIANA AT LAFAYETTE
LAFAYETTE, LOUISIANA
http://www.louisiana.edu
Medical Transcription Certificate Program
Administrative Medical Specialist Online Certificate Program
Travel Counselor Online Certificate Program

UNIVERSITY OF MAINE
ORONO, MAINE
http://www.umaine.edu
Certificate in Maine Studies
Certificate in Information Systems

UNIVERSITY OF VIRGINIA
CHARLOTTESVILLE, VIRGINIA
http://www.virginia.edu
Certificate in Criminal Justice
Editing
Electronic Publishing

VILLANOVA UNIVERSITY
VILLANOVA, PENNSYLVANIA
http://www.villanova.edu
Fundamentals of Project Management (online certificate program)

25 Certification Jobs

Following are profiles of 25 jobs that can be enhanced through
certification programs that take a year or less to complete.

■ Computer Service Technician

A computer service technician installs, repairs, and maintains computers and related equipment. Specific duties include servicing the mainframe, server, personal computer, disk drives, and printers. Other tasks include connecting equipment to power sources and communication lines, installing software and peripheral equipment, and checking components for correct configuration. Computer service technicians may also replace parts, conduct diagnostic tests, and conduct preventive maintenance.

MAY BE GOOD FOR YOU NOW IF YOU
■ Need experience or to complete an internship
■ Are good with computers and enjoy working with them
■ Like helping people
■ Enjoy working with your hands

HELPFUL PERSONAL TRAITS
■ Good communication skills
■ Analytical and logical
■ Able to solve problems
■ Able to work both independently and on a team
■ Work well under deadline pressure

VALUE TO YOUR CAREER DEVELOPMENT
■ Can help to meet the values of achievement, knowledge, skill, and helping others
■ Satisfaction derived from having solved a computer problem

VALUE TO EMPLOYER/SOCIETY
■ Computer systems and programs are vital to the operations of most American businesses
■ Can save businesses thousands of dollars through efficient repairs and quick restoration of service

POSSIBLE DOWNSIDES
■ May have to work in cramped and awkward positions
■ May involve lifting
■ Possible risk of electrocution

POPULATION GROUPS
- Single Parent
- Volunteer
- General

PREPARATION
- An associate's degree from an accredited institution is preferred
- Knowledge of electronics is helpful
- Certification strongly recommended and increasingly required
- Will need to keep up with changing technology by attending computer training sessions

CERTIFICATION
- A variety of certification programs are available from the International Society of Certified Electronics Technicians and the Institute for Certification of Computing Professionals, among other organizations.

RELATED JOBS/TITLES
- Data Processing Equipment Repairer
- Computer Repairer
- Computer Electronics Technician
- Computer Support Specialist
- Automated Teller Machine Servicer

EARNINGS
- $19,760 to $31,380 to $48,720

OUTLOOK
- According to the *Occupational Outlook Handbook,* jobs for computer service technicians are projected to grow as fast as the average through 2010. Opportunities are expected to be best for those with knowledge of electronics and experience in computer repairs.

FOR MORE INFORMATION

For information on internships, student membership, and the magazine, Crossroads, *contact:*

Association for Computing Machinery
One Astor Plaza
1515 Broadway
New York, NY 10036-5701
212-869-7440
sigs@acm.org
http://www.acm.org

For information on computer technology, employment, and certification, contact:

Computing Technology Industry Association
1815 South Meyers Road, Suite 300
Oakbrook Terrace, IL 60181-5228
630-268-1818
http://www.comptia.org

For career and placement information, contact:

Electronics Technicians Association
502 North Jackson Street
Greencastle, IN 46135
800-288-3824
eta@tds.net
http://www.eta-sda.com

For industry and certification information, contact the following organizations:

Institute for Certification of Computing Professionals
2350 East Devon Avenue, Suite 115
Des Plaines, IL 60018-4610
800-843-8227
office@iccp.org
http://www.iccp.org

International Society of Certified Electronics Technicians
3608 Pershing Avenue
Fort Worth, TX 76107-4527
817-921-9101
info@iscet.org
http://www.iscet.org

■ Computer Software Engineer

A computer software engineer applies the theories and techniques of computer science, engineering, and mathematical analysis to the design, development, testing, and evaluation of software systems. Software engineers set specifications, design and develop software, and program and customize software to meet the client's unique environment. Other tasks may include trouble-shooting, determining user needs, adjusting existing software, and maintaining an institution's computer system.

MAY BE GOOD FOR YOU NOW IF YOU

■ Want to work part-time or temporarily or be self-employed

■ Enjoy solving computer-related problems

■ Enjoy working on the creative side of computer technology

HELPFUL PERSONAL TRAITS

■ Analytical and alert

■ Able to work under pressure

■ Good communication skills

■ Creative

■ Computer-proficient

■ Able to cope with constant change

VALUE TO YOUR CAREER DEVELOPMENT

■ Can help meet the values of achievement, creativity, intellectual growth, knowledge, and skill

■ Satisfaction derived from being able to solve technical problems in a creative way

VALUE TO EMPLOYER/SOCIETY

■ Contributes to improving the work production and performance of businesses

■ Part of a highly valued occupational area

■ Development of new software may save employer significant cost and improve revenues

POSSIBLE DOWNSIDES

■ Pressure to meet deadlines

■ Vulnerable to eye strain and back, hand, and wrist problems

POPULATION GROUPS
- Part-Time/Temporary
- Single Parent
- Senior Citizen
- Job Complement
- Degree Complement
- General

PREPARATION
- Most employers require at least an associate's degree in computer engineering or programming
- A bachelor's degree along with strong background in computer systems and technologies is increasingly preferred
- A graduate degree is preferred for more challenging jobs
- Continuing education is necessary

CERTIFICATION
- Computer companies offer certification programs in their own software programs. The Institution for Certification of Computing Professionals and the Institute of Electrical and Electronics Engineers Computer Society are two of a number of organizations that offer voluntary certification.

RELATED JOBS/TITLES
- Systems Analyst
- Computer Scientist
- Computer Programmer
- Database Administrator
- Computer Software Designer

EARNINGS
- $42,710 to $67,670 to $106,680

OUTLOOK
- According to the *Occupational Outlook Handbook,* the field of software engineering is expected to be the fastest-growing occupation through 2010. While the need for software engineers will remain high, computer languages will probably change every few years, and software engineers will need to attend seminars and

workshops to learn new computer languages and software design.

FOR MORE INFORMATION

For information on internships, student membership, and the student magazine, Crossroads, *contact:*

Association for Computing Machinery
1515 Broadway
New York, NY 10036
800-342-6626
sigs@acm.org
http://www.acm.org

For certification information, contact:

Institute for Certification of Computing Professionals
2350 East Devon Avenue, Suite 115
Des Plaines, IL 60018-4610
800-843-8227
http://www.iccp.org

For information on scholarships, student membership, and the student newsletter, looking.forward, *contact:*

IEEE Computer Society
1730 Massachusetts Avenue, NW
Washington, DC 20036-1992
http://www.computer.org

For more information on careers in computer software, contact:

Software and Information Industry Association
1090 Vermont Avenue, NW, Sixth Floor
Washington, DC 20005
202-289-7442
http://www.siia.net

■ Claims Adjuster

A claims adjuster acts as an intermediary between an individual and a company (usually an insurance company) and is responsible for accepting claims, interpreting and explaining policies and regulations, and resolving disputes. Duties can include policy research, making decisions about coverage, authorizing payment referral to investigators, contacting claimants via phone or mail, acquiring information, consulting with other professionals, negotiating and settling claims, testifying in court, and writing reports.

MAY BE GOOD FOR YOU NOW IF YOU
- Desire to help those who have suffered personal, physical, or property damage
- Want to work out of your home
- Enjoy working with people and believe in fairness

HELPFUL PERSONAL TRAITS
- Able to make sound judgments
- Analytical
- Sensitive to the needs of others
- Objective and fair
- Honest
- Computer-proficient
- Good communication skills
- Conscientious

VALUE TO YOUR CAREER DEVELOPMENT
- Can help to meet the values of helping others, achievement, justice, and knowledge
- Satisfaction derived from contributing to the resolution of disputes

VALUE TO EMPLOYER/SOCIETY
- Helps insurance companies hold down unfair costs that may be due to claimant error or fraud
- Successful resolution of issues benefits both insurance companies and the people they insure

POSSIBLE DOWNSIDES

- May have to travel to places of disaster or damage sites, which may present risks
- May have to work weekends, evenings, and extra hours
- May have to contend with the assumption that you may not be fair or objective

POPULATION GROUPS

- Part-Time/Temporary
- General

PREPARATION

- College degree preferred
- Courses in business, accounting, and computers are helpful

CERTIFICATION

- Most states require licensing of claims representatives. The requirements for licensing vary and may include age restrictions, state residency, education in such classes as loss adjustment or insurance, character references, and written examinations. The Insurance Institute of America offers the Associate in Claims Certificate (AIC).

RELATED JOBS/TITLES

- Accountant
- Actuary
- Insurance Policy Processor
- Insurance Underwriter
- Insurance Agent or Broker
- Risk Manager

EARNINGS

- $25,030 to $41,080 to $68,130

OUTLOOK

- Growth of employment in claims adjusting will be about as fast as the average through 2010, according to the U.S. Department of Labor. Claims representatives who specialize in property and casualty insurance; health insurance; complex business insurance, such as marine cargo, workers' compensation, and product and pollution liability insurance, will be in demand.

FOR MORE INFORMATION

Information on health insurance adjusting and continuing education can be obtained from:

Health Insurance Association of America
555 13th Street, NW, Suite 500
Washington, DC 20004
202-824-1600
http://www.hiaa.org

For information on the Associate in Claims designation and other educational programs, contact:

Insurance Institute of America
720 Providence Road
PO Box 3016
Malvern, PA 19355-0716
800-644-2101
cserv@cpcuiia.org
http://www.aicpcu.org

For information on the Associate, Life and Health Claims, and the Fellow, Life Management Institute, designations, contact:

Life Office Management Association
2300 Windy Ridge Parkway, Suite 600
Atlanta, GA 30339-8443
800-275-5662
http://www.loma.org

Information on public insurance adjusting can be obtained from:

National Association of Public Insurance Adjusters
21165 Whitfield Place, #105
Potomac Falls, VA 20165
703-433-9217
napia@erols.com
http://www.napia.com

■ Certified Marketing Executive

Certified marketing executives (CME) supervise and coordinate the work of product developers and marketing managers. They conduct consumer-demand research, develop marketing strategies, find and develop new markets, and create pricing strategies for both existing and new products. They also work with advertising and promotion managers.

MAY BE GOOD FOR YOU NOW IF YOU

■ Desire to advance into the upper ranks of your profession

■ Want to increase potential for higher earnings

■ Want to improve the quality of your current job performance

HELPFUL PERSONAL TRAITS

■ Ambitious

■ Persuasive

■ Strong communication skills

■ Able to work under stress and meet deadlines

■ Tactful

■ Decisive

■ Proficient at speaking and writing

■ Good team player

VALUE TO YOUR CAREER DEVELOPMENT

■ Supports the values of achievement, recognition, and wealth

■ May help you acquire more authority and influence

VALUE TO EMPLOYER/SOCIETY

■ May help to improve employer's reputation and, as a result, increase customer demand

■ Can help ensure that products and services will meet customers' quality expectations

POSSIBLE DOWNSIDES

■ May experience high stress due to pressure to produce

■ Long hours and travel required

■ Possible job transfers

POPULATION GROUPS
- Job Complement
- Degree Complement

PREPARATION
- A bachelor's or master's degree and marketing experience are recommended

CERTIFICATION
- The Certified Marketing Executive (CME) designation is offered by Sales and Marketing Executives International

RELATED JOBS/TITLES
- Certified Sales Executive
- Certified Professional Salesperson
- Marketing Research Analyst
- Promotion Manager
- Advertising Manager
- Public Relations Manager

EARNINGS
- Marketing managers: $27,840 to $71,240 to $137,780
- Marketing research analysts: $37,030 to $51,190 to $96,360

OUTLOOK
- According to the *Occupational Outlook Handbook,* jobs for marketing managers are projected to increase faster than the average through 2010. Opportunities will be best for those with graduate degrees who seek employment in marketing research firms, financial services organizations, health care institutions, advertising firms, manufacturing firms producing consumer goods, and insurance companies.

FOR MORE INFORMATION

For information on college chapters, internship opportunities, and awards available, contact:

American Advertising Federation
1101 Vermont Avenue, NW, Suite 500
Washington, DC 20005-6306
202-898-0089
aaf@aaf.org
http://www.aaf.org

For information on agencies, contact:

American Association of Advertising Agencies
405 Lexington Avenue, 18th Floor
New York, NY 10174-1801
212-682-2500
http://www.aaaa.org

For career resources and job listings, contact or check out the following Web site:

American Marketing Association
311 South Wacker Drive, Suite 5800
Chicago, IL 60606
800-262-1150
http://www.marketingpower.com

For information on certification, education, and resources, contact:

Sales and Marketing Executives International
PO Box 1390
Sumas, WA 98295-1390
312-893-0751
http://www.smei.org

■ Certified Public Accountant

A certified public accountant (CPA) provides assistance to companies and individuals in maintaining accurate bookkeeping and financial records. Basic duties include preparing, analyzing, interpreting, and verifying financial documents. CPAs may specialize in such areas as public accounting, management, government accounting, internal auditing, and cost accounting. Some of the services that might be offered by CPAs include budget analysis, financial investment, asset management, consulting, tax preparation, preparing financial reports and statements, and evaluating accounts payable/receivable.

MAY BE GOOD FOR YOU NOW IF YOU
■ Have at least a bachelor's degree and have worked in accounting for a number of years
■ Have a strong desire to advance as far as possible in this field
■ Plan to start/expand your own business

HELPFUL PERSONAL TRAITS
■ Computer-proficient
■ Good at solving math problems
■ Able to explain complex financial data to others
■ High degree of integrity
■ Strong analytical skills

VALUE TO YOUR CAREER DEVELOPMENT
■ Can help meet the values of achievement, skill, knowledge, independence, and justice
■ Satisfaction derived from solving financial problems and helping individuals to become financially efficient

VALUE TO EMPLOYER/SOCIETY
■ May be instrumental in helping a company to realize cost savings by reducing waste and uncovering fraud
■ Can contribute to higher revenues by recommending wise investments
■ Can contribute to a company's reputation for efficiency

POSSIBLE DOWNSIDES

■ If self-employed, may have to work long hours during tax seasons

■ May have to meet short deadlines

■ Possibility of being involved with those who may be engaged in fraudulent practices

POPULATION GROUPS

■ Job Complement

■ Degree Complement

■ General

PREPARATION

■ Bachelor's degree in accounting or related field is recommended

■ Previous experience or a higher degree can be an advantage

■ Large public accounting firms prefer people with a master's degree in accounting

■ Certification required to become a CPA

CERTIFICATION

■ CPAs must pass a qualifying examination and hold a certificate issued by the state in which they practice. In most states, a college degree is required for admission to the CPA examinations; a few states allow candidates to substitute years of public accounting experience for the college degree requirement. Information is available from a state board of accountancy or from the American Institute of Certified Public Accountants (AICPA).

The Uniform CPA examination administered by the AICPA is used by all states.

Other credentials are also available, such as the Certified Management Accountant (CMA) designation offered by the Institute of Management Accounting. The Accreditation Council for Accountancy and Taxation confers the following three designations: Accredited Business Accountant or Accredited Business Advisor (ABA), Accredited Tax Preparer (ATP), and Accredited Tax Advisor (ATA). The Institute of Internal Auditors offers the Certified Internal Auditor (CIA) designation, and the Certified Information Systems Auditor (CISA) designation is offered by the Information Systems Audit and Control Association.

RELATED JOBS/TITLES
- Financial Analyst
- Accountant
- Tax Examiner
- Cost Estimator
- Financial Advisor
- Budget Analyst

EARNINGS
- $28,190 to $43,500 to $73,770

OUTLOOK
- According to the *Occupational Outlook Handbook,* jobs for accountants are projected to grow about as fast as the average through 2010. Accountants without college degrees will find more paraprofessional accounting positions, similar to the work of paralegals, as the number of lower- and mid-level workers expands. Demand will also be high for specialized accounting temps; CPA firms have started to hire temps to increase their staff during seasonal business cycles. Demand for recent college grads is falling as firms seek out experienced professionals with marketing savvy, proven sales ability, and international experience.

FOR MORE INFORMATION
For information on accreditation and testing, contact:

Accreditation Council for Accountancy and Taxation
1010 North Fairfax Street
Alexandria, VA 22314-1574
888-289-7763
info@acatcredentials.org
http://www.acatcredentials.org

For information on accredited programs in accounting, contact:

Association to Advance Collegiate Schools of Business
600 Emerson Road, Suite 300
St. Louis, MO 63141-6762
314-872-8481
http://www.aacsb.edu

For information about the Uniform CPA Examination and about becoming a student member, contact:

American Institute of Certified Public Accountants
1211 Avenue of the Americas
New York, NY 10036
memsat@aicpa.org
http://www.aicpa.org

For more information on women in accounting, contact:

Educational Foundation for Women in Accounting
PO Box 1925
Southeastern, PA 19399-1925
610-407-9229
http://www.efwa.org

For information on certification, contact:

Information Systems Audit and Control Association and Foundation
3701 Algonquin Road, Suite 1010
Rolling Meadows, IL 60008
847-253-1545
http://www.isaca.org

For information on internal auditing and the CIA designation, contact:

Institute of Internal Auditors
249 Maitland Avenue
Altamonte Springs, FL 32701-4201
407-830-7600
iia@theiia.org
http://www.theiia.org

For information about management accounting and the CMA designation, as well as student membership, contact:

Institute of Management Accountants
10 Paragon Drive
Montvale, NJ 07645-1718
800-638-4427
ima@imanet.org
http://www.imanet.org

■ Database Administrator

Database administrators specialize in the management of systems software. They organize and share data, establish requirements for users, set up databases, evaluate and coordinate changes, train new users, and ensure performance. Other tasks may include design supervision, security, planning, and database maintenance. Database administrators may advise companies on major decisions concerning computer purchases, system designs, and personnel training.

MAY BE GOOD FOR YOU NOW IF YOU
■ Want to work on a temporary basis or be self-employed

■ Enjoy challenges

■ Have extensive computer experience

HELPFUL PERSONAL TRAITS
■ Good communication skills

■ Detail-oriented

■ Analytical and logical

■ Organized

■ Good at solving problems, particularly technical problems

VALUE TO YOUR CAREER DEVELOPMENT
■ Can help meet the values of achievement, knowledge, wisdom, and recognition

■ Satisfaction derived from solving complex computer problems

■ Satisfaction derived from continually learning

■ High wages

VALUE TO EMPLOYER/SOCIETY
■ Efficient maintenance and security of databases helps protect information that, if lost or destroyed, could result in the loss of millions of dollars

■ Provides essential support to many other jobs

POSSIBLE DOWNSIDES
■ Long periods of time working at the computer may increase chances of developing back, hand, and wrist problems as well as eye strain

POPULATION GROUPS
■ Part-Time/Temporary

■ Single Parent

■ Job Complement

■ Degree Complement

■ General

PREPARATION
■ A bachelor's degree is increasingly required, although some employers may consider experience and proven expertise

■ Employers prefer the degree to be in computer science or management information systems

■ Co-ops and internships can enhance job possibilities

■ Certification can provide a competitive edge

CERTIFICATION
■ The Institute for Certification of Computing Professionals offers certification for database administrators. In addition, some database developers offer training and certification for users of their products. (See pages 182-183.)

RELATED JOBS/TITLES
■ Systems Administrator

■ Network Administrator

■ Computer and Information Systems Manager

■ Data Manager

■ Computer Software Engineer

■ Database Analyst

EARNINGS
■ $24,400 to $51,990 to $89,320

OUTLOOK
■ According to the *Occupational Outlook Handbook,* jobs for database administrators are projected to be among the fastest-growing occupations through 2010. Employment opportunities should be best in large urban areas because of the large numbers of businesses and organizations. However, smaller communities are also rapidly developing significant job opportunities, allow-

ing skilled workers to choose from a wide range of jobs throughout the country.

FOR MORE INFORMATION

For information on career opportunities or student chapters, contact:

Association of Information Technology Professionals
33405 Treasury Center
Chicago, IL 60694-3400
847-825-8124
aitp_hq@aitp.org
http://www.aitp.org

The Data Management Association (DAMA) International is an organization for professionals involved in business intelligence and data management. Visit its Web site to read articles related to these issues in DM Review.

DAMA International
PO Box 5786
Bellevue, WA 98006-5786
425-562-2636
DAMA@DAMA.org
http://www.dama.org

For information about scholarships, student membership, and careers, contact:

IEEE Computer Society
1730 Massachusetts Avenue, NW
Washington, DC 20036-1992
202-371-0101
http://www.computer.org

To read articles from the quarterly bulletin Data Engineering, *produced by the IEEE Technical Committee on Data Engineering, visit this Web site:*

Data Engineering
http://www.research.microsoft.com/research/db/debull/
issues-list.htm

For more information about computer certification, contact:

Institute for Certification of Computing Professionals
2350 East Devon Avenue, Suite 115
Des Plaines, IL 60018
800-843-8422
office@iccp.org
http://www.iccp.org

For more information on the Association for Computing Machinery's special interest group on management of data, visit the Web site:

Special Interest Group on Management of Data
http://www.acm.org/sigmod

■ Dental Assistant

A dental assistant provides assistance to dentists in patient care, office operations, and lab work. Most dental assistants work alongside the dentist as he or she treats patients. Responsibilities may include acquiring information from patients, adjusting seats for patients' comfort, preparing instruments for treatment, handing instruments and materials to the dentist, keeping the patient's mouth dry and clear, providing instructions to patient about upcoming treatment and oral health care, processing X-ray films, and making tooth impressions. Other duties may include removing sutures, applying anesthetics to gums, removing excess cement, inserting rubber clamps, and performing a variety of clerical and receptionist tasks.

MAY BE GOOD FOR YOU NOW IF YOU
- Want to work in a dental office
- Enjoy helping people
- Eventually want to become a dentist
- Desire to assist those who suffer from teeth-related problems
- Like challenges

HELPFUL PERSONAL TRAITS
- Good vision and manual dexterity
- Able to react quickly
- Able to maintain emotional composure
- Alert
- Dependable
- Organized
- Friendly

VALUE TO YOUR CAREER DEVELOPMENT
- Can help meet the values of helping and caring for others and health
- Satisfaction derived from having contributed to relieving patients' pain and knowing that your advice could help to prevent future problems

VALUE TO EMPLOYER/SOCIETY

- Provides invaluable help to dentists and frees them to do other tasks
- Helps to relieve suffering and pain for many patients

POSSIBLE DOWNSIDES

- Must wear protective garments, including masks, gloves, and eyewear, to prevent transmission of infectious diseases and bacteria
- Risks associated with working around radiographic equipment
- Must stand for long periods

POPULATION GROUPS

- Part-Time/Temporary
- Volunteer
- General

PREPARATION

- Skills usually are acquired on the job
- Associates' degree and certificate programs are offered at trade schools, technical institutes, and community and junior colleges and in the armed forces
- High school courses in health, biology, chemistry, and office practice are helpful
- Certification enhances employment possibilities

CERTIFICATION

- The Dental Assisting National Board offers voluntary certification as a certified dental assistant (CDA). In 21 states dental assistants are allowed to take X rays (under a dentist's direction) only after completing a precise training program and passing a test. Earning the CDA certification fulfills this requirement.

RELATED JOBS/TITLES

- Dental Receptionist
- Medical Assistant
- Pharmacy Technician
- Occupational Therapist Assistant

EARNINGS
■ $17,190 to $25,970 to $38,630

OUTLOOK
■ According to the *Occupational Outlook Handbook,* jobs for dental assistants are projected to grow much faster than the average through 2010. Dentists who earned their dental degrees since the 1970s are more likely than older dentists to hire one or more assistants. Also, as dentists increase their knowledge of innovative techniques such as implantology and periodontal therapy, they generally delegate more routine tasks to assistants so they can make the best use of their time and increase profits.

FOR MORE INFORMATION
For publications, information on dental schools, and scholarship information, contact:

American Dental Education Association
1625 Massachusetts Avenue, NW, Suite 600
Washington, DC 20036-2212
202-667-9433
adea@adea.org
http://www.adea.org

For continuing education information and career services, contact:

American Dental Assistants Association
203 North LaSalle Street, Suite 1320
Chicago, IL 60601-1225
312-541-1550
adaa1@aol.com
http://www.dentalassistant.org

For education information, contact:

American Dental Association
211 East Chicago Avenue
Chicago, IL 60611
312-440-2500
http://www.ada.org/index.html

For information on voluntary certification for dental assistants, contact:

Dental Assisting National Board
676 North Saint Clair, Suite 1880
Chicago, IL 60611
312-642-3368
danbmail@dentalassisting.com
http://www.dentalassisting.com

National Association of Dental Assistants
900 South Washington Street, Suite G13
Falls Church, VA 22046
703-237-8616

■ Desktop Publishing Specialist

Desktop publishing specialists use computer software to produce publications, including text, charts and graphs, photos, and various other graphics. Tasks may include editing, creating graphics and ads, scanning and altering photos, and designing page layouts. Products published can include books, cards, newsletters, newspapers, magazines, advertisements, direct mail, packaging, and tickets. The most common tools used are computers, scanners, and printers.

MAY BE GOOD FOR YOU NOW IF YOU
- Want to enter the publishing field
- Have done this type of work before and want to volunteer
- Have artistic ability
- Like working on computers

HELPFUL PERSONAL TRAITS
- Creative and imaginative
- Aptitude for spatial relationships
- Artistic
- Have a feel for design and form
- Good at following instructions

VALUE TO YOUR CAREER DEVELOPMENT
- Can help meet the values of creativity, achievement, recognition, and emotional well-being
- May fulfill a desire for self-expression

VALUE TO EMPLOYER/SOCIETY
- Can help save printing costs
- Reduces production times

POSSIBLE DOWNSIDES
- Pressure to meet deadlines
- May be prone to eye strain and back, hand, and wrist problems from long hours of computer work

POPULATION GROUPS
- Part-Time/Temporary
- Single Parent
- General

PREPARATION
- Postsecondary education is not required, but most employers require completion of a certificate program at a community or technical college in desktop publishing or technical and visual communications (usually a one-year program)
- Earning certification or an associate's degree is an advantage

CERTIFICATION
- The Association of Graphic Communications offers an Electronic Publishing Certificate that demonstrates competency in industry standards. Software developers offer certification in their graphics and page makeup programs. For example, Adobe offers certification in Illustrator, Acrobat, Pagemaker, and Photoshop.

RELATED JOBS/TITLES
- DTP Operator
- Compositor
- Electronic Publishing Specialist
- Layout Artist
- Designer
- Web Publication Designer
- Production Artist

EARNINGS
- $17,800 to $30,600 to $50,920

OUTLOOK
- According to the *Occupational Outlook Handbook,* desktop publishers are among the 10 fastest-growing occupations through 2010 and will continue to grow at a faster-than-average rate. Electronic and digital processes are replacing the manual processes and creating a demand for qualified desktop publishing experts to handle typesetting, page layout, design, and editorial tasks. Quark XPress, Adobe PageMaker, Macromedia

FreeHand, Adobe Illustrator, and Adobe Photoshop are some programs often used in desktop publishing. Specialists with experience in these and other software will be in demand.

FOR MORE INFORMATION
For career brochures and other information about grants, scholarships, and educational programs, contact the following organizations:

Association for Suppliers of Printing, Publishing, and Converting Technologies
1899 Preston White Drive
Reston, VA 20191-4367
703-264-7200
npes@npes.org
http://www.npes.org

Graphic Arts Technical Foundation
200 Deer Run Road
Sewickley, PA 15143-2600
800-910-GATF
info@gatf.org
http://www.gatf.org

Independent Computer Consultants Association
11131 South Towne Square, Suite F
St. Louis, MO 63123
800-774-4222
info@icca.org
http://www.icca.org

Society for Technical Communication
901 North Stuart Street, Suite 904
Arlington, VA 22203-1822
703-522-4114
stc@stc.org
http://www.stc.org

For additional information on the graphic arts industry, check the following Web site:

Graphic Arts Information Network
http://www.gain.org

■ Farm Manager

A farm manager directs and oversees the activities of one or more farms or ranches. Tasks vary depending on the crops grown (grain, cotton, fruit, vegetables, etc.) or livestock raised (beef or dairy cattle, pigs, poultry, etc.). Crop farm managers supervise planning, tilling, planting, fertilizing, cultivating, spraying, and harvesting. Livestock farm managers oversee planning, breeding, buying and selling, feeding, watering, milking, sanitation, and disease prevention.

Other responsibilities of farm managers may include hiring, supervising, purchasing supplies, staying abreast of laws, preparing for weather conditions, meeting with other farmers, managing finances, and maintaining equipment and property (including facilities and structures).

MAY BE GOOD FOR YOU NOW IF YOU

■ Grew up on a farm and appreciate hard, physical work

■ Are familiar with agricultural techniques and applications

■ Want to be self-employed

■ Currently work on your family farm and plan to eventually take it over

HELPFUL PERSONAL TRAITS

■ Like working outdoors

■ Good business sense

■ Observant

■ Able to make sound judgments

■ Able to manage and supervise

■ Patient

VALUE TO YOUR CAREER DEVELOPMENT

■ Can help meet the values of achievement, health, helping others, and independence

■ Satisfaction derived from working the land and having a successful crop year

■ Satisfaction derived from contributing to the worldwide food supply

VALUE TO EMPLOYER/SOCIETY

- American farmers are responsible for feeding the country and much of the world
- Provides services, products, and expertise that American society cannot live without

POSSIBLE DOWNSIDES

- Small-farm managers may have to engage in hard, strenuous work in addition to management tasks
- Increasing competition to stay in business can create high stress
- Farms usually have to become larger to stay in business
- May not receive deserved respect or needed compensation

POPULATION GROUPS

- General
- Degree Complement
- Job Complement

PREPARATION

- A bachelor's or master's degree is required in some areas of agriculture
- Several years of successful farm management experience are required for certification
- Continued education is a must in order to stay abreast of new trends and technologies

CERTIFICATION

The American Society of Farm Managers and Rural Appraisers offers voluntary certification as an accredited farm manager (AFM). Certification requires several years of experience working on a farm, an academic background (a bachelor's or preferably a master's degree in a branch of agricultural science), and courses covering the business, financial, and legal aspects of farm management.

RELATED JOBS/TITLES
▪ Agriculture Manager

▪ Farm Owner

▪ Livestock Farmer

▪ Rancher

EARNINGS
▪ $18,790 to $32,090 to $55,370

OUTLOOK
▪ According to the *Occupational Outlook Handbook*, jobs for farm managers are projected to grow slower than the average through 2010. Some trends that farmers may follow in their efforts to increase income include more diversified crop production; for example, farmers may choose to plant high-oil or high-protein corn, which bring more money in the marketplace. But these new grains also require different methods of storage and marketing. Some small-scale farmers have found opportunities in organic food production, farmers' markets, and similar market niches that require more direct personal contact with their customers.

FOR MORE INFORMATION
For resources and information on education programs and certification, contact:

American Society of Farm Managers and Rural Appraisers
950 Cherry Street, Suite 508
Denver, CO 80222
http://www.asfmra.org

Center for Rural Affairs
PO Box 406
Walthill, NE 68067
http://www.cfra.org

The AFBF Web site features legislative news, state farm bureau news, online brochures, and information on Farm Bureau Programs such as AFBF Young Farmers & Ranchers Program. This program, for those age 18 to 35, offers educational conferences, networking opportunities, and competitive events.

American Farm Bureau Federation (AFBF)
225 Touhy Avenue
Park Ridge, IL 60068
847-685-8858
http://www.fb.org

To learn about farmer-owner cooperatives and how cooperative businesses operate, contact:

National Council of Farmer Cooperatives
50 F Street, NW, Suite 900
Washington, DC 20001
202-626-8700
http://www.ncfc.org

For information on farm policies, homeland security issues, and other news relating to the agricultural industry, visit the USDA Web site.

U.S. Department of Agriculture (USDA)
Washington, DC 20250
202-720-2791
http://www.usda.gov

■ Financial Analyst

A financial analyst provides investment analysis and guidance to businesses and individuals. Duties include assessing economic performance of companies and industries; gathering and analyzing financial information; making investment recommendations and explaining options; maintaining familiarity with companies' financial statements and commodity prices, sales, costs, expenses, and tax rates to determine value and future earning potential; consulting with other company officials; and researching and maintaining knowledge of business and industry trends, regulations, and policies. Financial analysts use spreadsheets and statistical software and spend significant time writing reports and making presentations.

MAY BE GOOD FOR YOU NOW IF YOU
■ Desire to be self-employed

■ Want a high income

■ Are good at anticipating economic trends and making predictions

■ Need challenges

HELPFUL PERSONAL TRAITS
■ Good writing and reading comprehension skills

■ Able to clearly explain complex financial concepts

■ Logical and analytical

■ Strong communication skills

■ Computer-proficient

■ Independent

■ Observant and alert

■ Able to make sound judgments

VALUE TO YOUR CAREER DEVELOPMENT
■ May help to meet the values of wealth, achievement, competition, and knowledge

■ Satisfaction derived when your advice yields positive results

VALUE TO EMPLOYER/SOCIETY

- Can help to expand a company and increase revenues
- Recommendations of sound investment decisions may create more jobs

POSSIBLE DOWNSIDES

- Pressure to meet deadlines
- Sometimes have to work long hours
- May not accurately foresee sudden economic swings that adversely affect investment recommendations
- May require travel

POPULATION GROUPS

- Degree Complement
- Job Complement
- General

PREPARATION

- Bachelor's degree required
- Background in business administration, accounting, economics, finance, or statistics is usually required
- Certification improves competitive edge

CERTIFICATION

- The Association of Investment Management and Research offers certification as a Chartered Financial Analyst (CFA). The CFA charter is recognized around the world as a standard in the finance industry. Many employers expect job seekers to be CFA charterholders. For certain upper-level positions, some firms require that you have a Certified Public Accountant (CPA) license.

RELATED JOBS/TITLES

- Investment Analyst
- Financial Consultant
- Security Analyst
- Financial Planner
- Financial Advisor

EARNINGS

▪ $31,880 to $52,420 to $101,760

OUTLOOK

▪ According to the *Occupational Outlook Handbook,* jobs for financial analysts are projected to increase faster than the average through 2010. International securities markets, the complexity of financial products, and business mergers and acquisitions will create a demand for financial analysts to sort through all the issues involved. Because of the close scrutiny analysts have been under, it is increasingly desirable for financial analysts to hold the CFA charter.

FOR MORE INFORMATION

This organization's Web site offers an e-library containing a helpful dictionary of financial terminology. Industry news and certification information are also available.

Association for Financial Professionals
7315 Wisconsin Avenue, Suite 600 West
Bethesda, MD 20814
301-907-2862
http://www.afponline.org

For complete AIMR information, including lists of AIMR societies, publications, news, conference details, and certification information, contact:

Association for Investment Management and Research (AIMR)
PO Box 3668
560 Ray C. Hunt Drive
Charlottesville, VA 22903-0668
800-247-8132
info@aimr.org
http://www.aimr.org

The NYSSA Web site includes a list of top employers of financial analysts as well as an article on becoming a security analyst.

New York Society of Security Analysts (NYSSA)
1601 Broadway, 11th Floor
New York, NY 10019-7406
800-248-0108
http://www.nyssa.org

For information on laws and regulations pertaining to investors and the securities markets, contact:

U.S. Securities and Exchange Commission
Office of Investor Education and Assistance
450 Fifth Street, NW
Washington, DC 20549
202-942-7040
help@sec.gov
http://www.sec.gov/

This Web site has links to financial, investment, and security analyst societies.

AnalystForum
http://www.analystforum.com

■ Global Career Development Facilitator

Service providers who have earned the Global Career Development Facilitator (GCDF) certification assist people who are seeking jobs, making career transitions, trying to choose a suitable college major, or determining a career or life direction.

Specific job responsibilities vary depending on the work setting. Most GCDFs help with client intake, screening, and referral. They assist with career decision-making and exploration, orientation, administration and scoring of career assessments, securing confidential materials, organizing and distributing career materials, assisting clients with computerized career guidance information and Internet research, preparing career displays, presenting workshops and seminars, maintaining career files, and performing clerical duties.

MAY BE GOOD FOR YOU NOW IF YOU

- Are in a school, college, or agency program that requires you to provide career development services but professional career counseling is limited or not available
- Desire to help people appropriately direct their lives
- Want to acquire career development skills to improve or expand your current services
- Seek recognition for career-direction experiences and skills

HELPFUL PERSONAL TRAITS

- Computer-proficient
- Good communication skills
- Good listener
- Able to perform multiple tasks simultaneously
- Able to work independently and on a team
- Compassionate
- Trustworthy
- Organized

VALUE TO YOUR CAREER DEVELOPMENT

- Supports the values of helping and serving others
- Provides experience for future work in the helping professions

■ Provides knowledge and strategies you can use throughout your life to enrich personal development

VALUE TO EMPLOYER/SOCIETY

■ The knowledge and skills you teach can help others realize their career development goals

■ Helps employers meet job-training requirements and helps educators comply with governmental guidelines

■ Helps students and adults make better decisions

POSSIBLE DOWNSIDES

■ Further education and training is necessary to provide comprehensive, in-depth career direction

■ Must be supervised by a qualified professional counselor, and the availability of these professionally certified career counselors is limited

POPULATION GROUPS

■ Job Complement

■ Degree Complement

■ General

PREPARATION

■ Global Career Development Facilitator (GCDF) certification training programs are available at the postsecondary level or after you have earned an associate's, bachelor's, master's, or doctoral degree, as long as you meet the career development experience requirement

CERTIFICATION

■ GCDF certification is available from the Center for Credentialing and Education. Certification requires 120 hours of classroom training along with field experience.

RELATED JOBS/TITLES

■ Job Search Trainer

■ Career Development Case Manager

■ Career Specialist

■ Career Technician

■ Career Coach

- Career Resource Assistant
- Career Development Technician
- Career Center Coordinator

EARNINGS
- Specific salary information is not available for GCDFs
- Educational, vocational, and school counselors: $23,560 to $42,110 to $67,170

OUTLOOK
- Growth in the field of employment counseling should be faster than the average through 2010, according to the U.S. Department of Labor. One reason for this growth is increased school enrollments, even at the college level, which means more students are in need of the services of career counselors. Opportunities should also be available in government agencies as many states institute welfare-to-work programs or simply cut welfare benefits. In addition, laid-off workers, those re-entering the workforce, and those looking for second careers all create a need for the skills of career and employment counselors.

FOR MORE INFORMATION
For a variety of career resources for career seekers and career counseling professionals, contact the following organizations:

American Counseling Association
5999 Stevenson Avenue
Alexandria, VA 22304-3300
800-347-6647
http://www.counseling.org

Career Planning and Adult Development Network
PO Box 1484
Pacifica, CA 94044
650-359-6911
network@psctr.com
http://www.careernetwork.org

For information on the GCDF certification, contact:

Center for Credentialing and Education, Inc.
3 Terrace Way, Suite A
Greensboro, NC 27403
336-482-2856
http://www.cce-global.org

For resume and interview tips, general career information, and advice from the experts, contact or visit the following Web site:

National Association of Colleges and Employers (NACE)
62 Highland Avenue
Bethlehem, PA 18017-9085
800-544-5272
http://www.naceweb.org

For information on certification, contact:

National Board for Certified Counselors
PO Box 651051
Charlotte, NC 28265-1051
336-547-0607
nbcc@nbcc.org
http://www.nbcc.org

For more information on career counselors, contact:

National Career Development Association
10820 East 45th Street, Suite 210
Tulsa, OK 74146
918-663-7060
http://ncda.org

■ Human Resources Manager

A human resources manager oversees a company's or institution's employee hiring, departures, training and staff development, benefits, and policies. Other job tasks may include the development and coordination of personnel programs, researching benefit programs and policies, responding to and resolving employee issues, writing job descriptions and reports, meeting with department supervisors, and assisting with contract negotiations.

MAY BE GOOD FOR YOU NOW IF YOU

■ Have worked in a human resources department before

■ Have served in the past as a labor union official

■ Are experienced in this area and believe you could bring about positive change

HELPFUL PERSONAL TRAITS

■ Good listener

■ Fair

■ Patient

■ Sensitive

■ Able to work well individually and on a team

■ Excellent communication and negotiating skills

■ Aptitude for leadership

■ Broad background of knowledge

■ Computer-proficient

■ Able to work with diverse populations

■ Work well under pressure

■ Good at resolving conflicts

VALUE TO YOUR CAREER DEVELOPMENT

■ Can help meet the values of achievement, helping others, leadership, justice, and wealth

■ Satisfaction derived from policy changes you have helped enact

■ Satisfaction derived from resolving conflicts

VALUE TO EMPLOYER/SOCIETY

- Satisfied managers and employees often translate into a more positive work environment, which can lead to a higher quality of service or product, a better company reputation, and increased business and revenues

POSSIBLE DOWNSIDES

- May need to travel and work long hours
- Employee issues can be quite challenging and increase stress levels

POPULATION GROUPS

- Job Complement
- General

PREPARATION

- A college degree is preferred, especially one in human resources or labor relations
- A graduate degree is required for some specializations
- Certification may enhance advancement possibilities

CERTIFICATION

- Some membership organizations offer voluntary certifications. For example, the International Foundation of Employee Benefits Plans offers the Certified Employee Benefits Specialist certification to candidates who complete a series of college-level courses and pass exams on employee benefit plans. The Human Resources Certification Institute of the Society for Human Resources Management offers certification as a Professional in Human Resources or a Senior Professional in Human Resources. Both require experience and the passing of a comprehensive exam.

RELATED JOBS/TITLES

- Human Resource Director
- Personnel Manager
- Human Resource Specialist
- Employee Relations Manager
- Labor Relations Specialist

EARNINGS

■ $33,360 to $59,000 to $104,020

OUTLOOK

■ According to the *Occupational Outlook Handbook,* jobs for human resource managers are projected to grow about as fast as the average through 2010. Competition for jobs will continue to be strong, however, as there will be an abundance of qualified applicants. Opportunities will be best in the private sector and with consulting firms who offer personnel services to businesses that cannot afford to have their own extensive staffs.

FOR MORE INFORMATION

For information on standards and procedures in arbitration, contact:

American Arbitration Association
335 Madison Avenue, 10th Floor
New York, NY 10017
212-716-5800
http://www.adr.org

For news and information on compensation and benefits administration, contact:

American Compensation Association
14040 Northsight Boulevard
Scottsdale, AZ 85260
877-951-9191
customerrelations@worldatwork.org
http://www.worldatwork.org

For information on personnel careers in the health care industry, contact:

American Society for Healthcare Human Resources Administration
One North Franklin Street
Chicago, IL 60606
312-422-3725
ashhra@aha.org
http://www.ashhra.org

For information on careers in training, related industry links, and other resources, contact:

American Society for Training and Development
1640 King Street, Box 1443
Alexandria, VA 22313-2043
703-683-8100
http://www.astd.org

For a list of U.S. and Canadian schools offering degrees in industrial relations and human resource degree programs, contact:

Industrial Relations Research Association
121 Labor and Industrial Relations
University of Illinois, Urbana-Champaign
504 East Armory, MC-504
Champaign, IL 61820
irra@uiuc.edu
http://www.irra.uiuc.edu

For information on training, job opportunities, human resources publications, or online discussions, contact:

International Personnel Management Association
1617 Duke Street
Alexandria, VA 22314
703-549-7100
ipma@ipma-hr.org
http://www.ipma-hr.org

For information on career development and certification, contact:

Society for Human Resources Management
Human Resources Certification Institute
1800 Duke Street
Alexandria, VA 22314
703-548-3440
http://www.shrm.org
http://www.hrci.org/index.html

■ Medical Assistant

Medical assistants perform routine administrative and clinical tasks for health care professionals. Responsibilities can include providing information to patients, recording medical history, preparing patients for examinations and procedures, taking vital signs, changing dressings, and removing sutures. Medical assistants also collect and prepare lab tests, conduct electrocardiograms, draw blood, give injections, and perform a variety of clerical tasks.

MAY BE GOOD FOR YOU NOW IF YOU

■ Desire to interact with and serve others in a direct way

■ Want or need to have exposure to a medical environment

■ Have worked in an office environment before

HELPFUL PERSONAL TRAITS

■ Good communication skills

■ Computer-proficient

■ Patient

■ Friendly

■ Accurate and detail-oriented

VALUE TO YOUR CAREER DEVELOPMENT

■ Can meet the values of love, health, and serving others

■ May help you fulfill an interest in public health and safety

■ Supports a sensitivity to the physical needs of others

VALUE TO EMPLOYER/SOCIETY

■ Provides an important public relations and support service for physicians and other health professionals, which can be a key to whether patients continue to seek medical services

POSSIBLE DOWNSIDES

■ May work in an office that lacks sufficient help and thus have a heavy workload and stress

■ May not be appropriately recognized by professional staff

■ Heightened stress from being asked to perform multiple tasks in a short period

POPULATION GROUPS
- Single Parent
- Senior Citizen
- Part-Time/Temporary

PREPARATION
- Employers prefer completion of a one-year postsecondary medical assisting program

CERTIFICATION
- Voluntary certification is available through several agencies and organizations. The registered medical assistant (RMA) credential is awarded by American Medical Technologists, and the American Association of Medical Assistants awards a credential for certified medical assistant (CMA).

  Medical assistants generally do not need to be licensed, but some states require you to pass a test or take a course before you can do certain tasks, such as taking X rays.

RELATED JOBS/TITLES
- Medical Secretary
- Pharmacy Technician
- Medical Records Clerk
- Dental Assistant
- Occupational Therapist Aide
- Physical Therapist Aide
- Hospital Admitting Clerk

EARNINGS
- $16,700 to $23,000 to $32,850

OUTLOOK
- According to the *Occupational Outlook Handbook,* jobs for medical assistants are expected to be among the 10 fastest-growing occupations through 2010. Most openings will occur as a result of high turnover, but many will be the result of a predicted surge in the number of physicians' offices, clinics, and other outpatient care facilities. Experienced and formally trained medical assistants are preferred by many physicians. Word-processing

skills, other computer skills, and formal certification are all definite assets.

FOR MORE INFORMATION
For information on accreditation and testing, contact:

Accrediting Bureau of Health Education Schools
803 West Broad Street, Suite 730
Falls Church, VA 22046
703-533-2082
abhes@erols.com
http://www.abhes.org

For information on a career as a medical assistant, contact the following organizations:

American Association of Medical Assistants
20 North Wacker Drive, Suite 1575
Chicago, IL 60606-2963
312-899-1500
http://www.aama-ntl.org

American Medical Technologists
710 Higgins Road
Park Ridge, IL 60068-5765
847-823-5169
amtmail@aol.com
http://www.amt1.com

American Society of Podiatric Medical Assistants
2124 South Austin Boulevard
Cicero, IL 60804
888-882-7762
http://www.aspma.org

■ Medical Information Technician

A medical information technician organizes, evaluates, and maintains health information acquired by other health professionals about their patients. Tasks may include accurately recording and maintaining of medical charts, making sure necessary forms are completed correctly, entering information into the computer, obtaining clarification or adding information provided by physicians, assigning codes to diagnoses or procedures, consulting manuals, and tabulating and analyzing data for use in research.

MAY BE GOOD FOR YOU NOW IF YOU

- Enjoy working with detailed information
- Have previously worked in this area
- Plan to become a medical information manager

HELPFUL PERSONAL TRAITS

- Able to easily understand and interpret data
- Observant
- Detail-oriented
- Dependable
- Discreet
- Organized
- Good at repetition
- Analytical
- Comfortable using computers

VALUE TO YOUR CAREER DEVELOPMENT

- Can help meet the values of achievement, skill, and knowledge
- Satisfaction derived from knowing your work helps to maintain efficiency and minimize costs

VALUE TO EMPLOYER/SOCIETY

- Helps medical institutions comply with legal requirements
- Ensures that hospitals and medical offices have accurately identified services rendered and revenues owed
- Helps maintain the vast array of information necessary for physicians to properly diagnose and treat patients

POSSIBLE DOWNSIDES

■ May be subject to eye strain, muscle and back strain, or hand and wrist injuries due to long periods of time working on computers

POPULATION GROUPS

■ Degree Complement

■ General

PREPARATION

■ High school courses in anatomy, physiology, health, biology, chemistry, and computers are helpful

■ Usually requires completion of an associate's degree program accredited by the American Medical Association's Commission on Accreditation of Allied Health Professions (CAAHP) and the American Health Information Management Association (AHIMA)

■ Individuals with experience in certain related activities are eligible for an independent study program offered by AHIMA

■ Certification enhances chances for advancement

CERTIFICATION

■ Medical information technicians who have completed an accredited training program are eligible to take a national qualifying examination to earn the credential of registered health information technician (RHIT). The RHIT credential signifies that the technician has met the standards established by the American Health Information Management Association.

RELATED JOBS/TITLES

■ Medical Transcriptionist

■ Health Information Coder

■ Medical Records Technician

■ Medical Records Coder

■ Coding Specialist

EARNINGS

■ $15,710 to $22,750 to $35,170

OUTLOOK

■ According to the *Occupational Outlook Handbook*, jobs for medical information technicians are projected to grow much faster than the average through 2010. This expectation is related to the health care needs of a population that is both growing and aging and the trend toward more technologically sophisticated medicine and greater use of diagnostic procedures. It is also related to the increased requirements of regulatory bodies, insurance companies, and courts that scrutinize both costs and quality of care of health care providers. Technicians with associate's degrees and RHIT certification will have the best prospects, and the importance of such qualifications is likely to increase.

FOR MORE INFORMATION

For information on earnings, careers in health information management, and accreditation, contact:

American Health Information Management Association
PO Box 77-3081
Chicago, IL 60678-3081
312-233-1100
info@ahima.org
http://www.ahima.org

For a list of schools offering accredited programs in health information management, contact:

Commission on Accreditation of
Allied Health Education Programs
35 East Wacker Drive, Suite 1970
Chicago, IL 60601-2208
312-553-9355
caahep@caahep.org
http://www.caahep.org

■ Medical Laboratory Technician

Medical laboratory technicians usually work under the direction of medical and clinical laboratory technologists or laboratory managers. They are part of a team of specialists who examine and analyze body fluids, tissues, and cells using test tubes and other glassware and precision equipment, such as microscopes and automated blood analyzers. Duties may include preparing slides and specimens, operating and maintaining equipment, and performing tests and procedures. Some may cut and stain tissue specimens (histology) or collect blood samples (phlebotomy).

MAY BE GOOD FOR YOU NOW IF YOU
■ Have worked in a medical lab before

■ Plan to become a laboratory technologist

■ Have retired from this area and want to volunteer

HELPFUL PERSONAL TRAITS
■ Accurate and detail-oriented

■ Analytical

■ Work well under pressure

■ Good vision and color recognition

■ Team player

■ Computer-proficient

VALUE TO YOUR CAREER DEVELOPMENT
■ Can help meet the values of health and safety, knowledge, wisdom, intellectual growth, and helping others

■ Satisfaction derived from accurately identifying a disease that could present a serious health problem

VALUE TO EMPLOYER/SOCIETY
■ Extremely important to the correct detection, diagnosis, and treatment of diseases

■ May have a critical role in responding to the increasing possibility of chemical and biological terrorist threat

■ Contributes to public health and safety

POSSIBLE DOWNSIDES

- Must follow safety precautions, including wearing protective clothing, to avoid contracting infectious diseases
- Must stand for long periods

POPULATION GROUPS

- General
- Volunteer
- Senior Citizen

PREPARATION

- The minimum requirement is usually an associate's degree or certificate from an accredited school
- Many skills are learned on the job
- Certification is normally required for both entry and advancement
- Some states require licensing

CERTIFICATION

- Those who have earned an associate's degree are eligible for certification from several different agencies. You may become a certified Medical Laboratory Technician (MLT) by the Board of Registry of the American Society of Clinical Pathologists or the American Medical Technologists. In addition, the National Credentialing Agency for Laboratory Personnel offers certification for Clinical Laboratory Technicians (CLTs).

RELATED JOBS/TITLES

- Science Technician
- Clinical Lab Technician
- Lab Technician
- Chemical Technician
- Veterinary Technician

EARNINGS

- $18,550 to $27,540 to $42,370

OUTLOOK

▪ According to the *Occupational Outlook Handbook,* jobs for medical lab technicians are projected to grow about as fast as the average through 2010. Competition for jobs, however, may be strong. Opportunities will be best for well-trained technicians who are flexible in accepting responsibilities and willing to continue their education throughout their careers.

FOR MORE INFORMATION

For information on careers, certification, and continuing education, contact the following organizations:

American Medical Technologists
710 Higgins Road
Park Ridge, IL 60068-5765
847-823-5169
mail@amt1.com
http://www.amt1.com

American Society for Clinical Laboratory Science
7910 Woodmont Avenue, Suite 530
Bethesda, MD 20814
301-657-2768
http://www.ascls.org

For information on certification, contact:

American Society for Clinical Pathology Board of Registry
2100 West Harrison Street
Chicago, IL 60612
http://www.ascp.org/bor

American Association of Bioanalysts
917 Locust Street, Suite 1100
St. Louis, MO 63101-1419
314-241-1445
aab@aab.org
http://www.aab.org

National Credentialing Agency for Laboratory Personnel
PO Box 15945-289
Lenexa, KS 66285
913-438-5110, ext. 647
nca-info@goamp.com
http://www.nca-info.org

■ Optician

An optician follows prescriptions written by ophthalmologists or optometrists to design and fit patients with either eyeglasses or contact lenses. Duties usually include correctly interpreting and verifying prescriptions, making recommendations to customers, taking eye measurements, consulting with customers about past vision history, and preparing work orders. Some opticians perform technician tasks, such as grinding, polishing, and inserting lenses into frames; shaping or bending frames for proper fit; providing instructions to customers; and record-keeping.

MAY BE GOOD FOR YOU NOW IF YOU
■ Have a strong interest in the care and health of eyesight

■ Want to eventually become an optometrist or ophthalmologist

HELPFUL PERSONAL TRAITS
■ Good eye-hand coordination and manual dexterity

■ Good spatial perception

■ Good with detail and precision work

■ Courteous

■ Tactful

■ Friendly

VALUE TO YOUR CAREER DEVELOPMENT
■ Can help meet the values of achievement, health, skill, recognition, and helping others

■ Satisfaction derived from customer appreciation

VALUE TO EMPLOYER/SOCIETY
■ Contributes to providing vision care for millions of Americans

■ Helps to enhance and complement the physical appearance of customers

POSSIBLE DOWNSIDES
■ Requires standing for long periods

■ Risk of injury from glass cuts, chemical spills, or machine-related accidents

POPULATION GROUPS
- Single Parent
- General

PREPARATION
- Most receive on-the-job training
- Apprenticeship programs are offered by optical dispensing companies
- Two-year associate's degree programs are offered at community colleges and trade schools
- Background in physics, anatomy, algebra, geometry, and mechanical drawing are an advantage, as is past experience as a machinist
- Certification improves employment possibilities

CERTIFICATION
- More than 20 states currently require licensing of dispensing opticians. Contact the licensing board of the state or states in which you plan to work. Some states may permit dispensing opticians to fit contact lenses without certification, provided they have additional training. Voluntary certification is offered by the American Board of Opticianry and the National Contact Lens Examiners.

RELATED JOBS/TITLES
- Dispensing Optician
- Jeweler
- Ophthalmic Technician
- Watch Repairer
- Camera Equipment Repairer

EARNINGS
- $15,910 to $24,430 to $39,660

OUTLOOK
- According to the *Occupational Outlook Handbook,* jobs for opticians are projected to increase about as fast as the average through 2010. Employment opportunities should be especially good in larger urban areas because of the greater number of

retail optical stores. Those with an associate's degree in opticianry should be most successful in finding employment.

FOR MORE INFORMATION

For information on certification, contact:

American Board of Opticianry/National
Contact Lens Examiners
6506 Loisdale Road, Suite 209
Springfield, VA 22150
703-719-5800
http://www.ncleabo.org

For information on education and training programs, contact the following organizations:

Commission on Opticianry Accreditation
7023 Little River Turnpike, Suite 207
Annandale, VA 22003
703-941-9110
coa@erols.com
http://www.coaccreditation.com

National Academy of Opticianry
8401 Corporate Drive, Suite 605
Landover, MD 20785
800-229-4828
http://www.nao.org

Opticians Association of America
7023 Little River Turnpike, Suite 207
Annandale, VA 22003
703-916-8856
oaa@oaa.org
http://www.oaa.org

■ Orthotist/Prosthetist

Orthotists and prosthetists are distinct but related occupations. An orthotist builds, fits, adjusts, maintains, and repairs braces, footwear, neck collars, joint supports, and arch supports. A prosthetist constructs, fits, and repairs artificial limbs for individuals who have lost limbs due to illness or injury. Both orthotists and prosthetists read and fill prescriptions, examine patients, take measurements, make casts, cut and mold plastics and other materials, construct devices or limbs, fit devices or limbs to the patient, make adjustments, and provide instructions to patients.

MAY BE GOOD FOR YOU NOW IF YOU
■ Have served as a helper in this area previously

■ Desire to help those who have physical disabilities

■ Are good with your hands

HELPFUL PERSONAL TRAITS
■ Supportive and caring

■ Able to work both independently and on a team

■ Physical stamina

■ Manual dexterity

■ Creative

■ Industrious

■ Empathetic

■ Patient

■ Accurate

■ Detail-oriented

VALUE TO YOUR CAREER DEVELOPMENT
■ Can help meet the values of wisdom, helping others, skill, achievement, and recognition

■ Satisfaction derived from patients' appreciation and gratitude

VALUE TO EMPLOYER/SOCIETY
■ Gives patients confidence and hope as they cope with difficult changes

■ Enables people with physical disabilities to have mobility and function effectively

POSSIBLE DOWNSIDES
- May be dirty, noisy, and hot
- Risk of injuries from working with power and hand tools and heated plastics and metals
- Frustrations due to complications with fittings

POPULATION GROUPS
- General

PREPARATION
- A bachelor's degree is required. If your degree is in a subject other than prosthetics or orthotics, you must complete a one-year certificate program after college.
- A one-year residency is usually required after completing your educational program
- Prior work in health care as a machinist or model maker is helpful
- Working alongside a specialist is advisable

CERTIFICATION
- Certification is recommended. The American Board for Certification in Orthotics and Prosthetics grants three credentials: Certified Orthotist (CO), Certified Prosthetist (CP), and Certified Prosthetist/Orthotist (CPO). Licensing is required for orthotists and prosthetists in some states.

RELATED JOBS/TITLES
- Medical Appliance Technician
- Prosthetist Practitioner
- Orthotist Practitioner
- Physical Science Technician
- Dental Technician

EARNINGS
- $21,630 to $45,740 to $83,810

OUTLOOK
- According to the *Occupational Outlook Handbook,* jobs for orthotist/prosthetists are projected to grow about as fast as the average through 2010. Advancements in technology and new,

lightweight materials will require individuals who can design and fabricate attractive orthoses and prostheses.

FOR MORE INFORMATION

For news related to the field and education, visit this academy's Web site.

American Academy of Orthotists and Prosthetists
526 King Street, Suite 201
Alexandria, VA 22314
703-836-0788
http://www.oandp.org

For information on becoming a certified orthotist or prosthetist, contact:

American Board for Certification in Orthotics and Prosthetics
330 John Carlyle Street, Suite 210
Alexandria, VA 22314
703-836-7114
http://www.opoffice.org

For career and education information, contact:

American Orthotic and Prosthetic Association
330 John Carlyle Street, Suite 200
Alexandria, VA 22314
703-836-7116
info@aopanet.org
http://www.aopanet.org

For information on certification, contact:

Board for Orthotist/Prosthetist Certification
506 West Fayette Street
Century Building, Suite 200
Baltimore, MD 21201
410-539-3910
info@bocusa.org
http://www.bocusa.org

For information on accredited schools:

National Commission on Orthotic and Prosthetic Education
330 John Carlyle Street, Suite 200
Alexandria, VA 22314
703-836-7114
http://www.ncope.org

■ Pharmacy Technician

Pharmacy technicians help pharmacists provide medication and other health-related products to customers. Duties usually include receiving and checking prescriptions, counting and labeling bottles, referring orders to pharmacists, providing patients with ordered prescriptions (if working in a hospital setting, they may actually deliver medication to patients' rooms), reading charts, and stocking supplies. Other tasks include helping to mix drugs, maintaining equipment and clean work areas, stocking shelves, operating the cash register, and maintaining records.

MAY BE GOOD FOR YOU NOW IF YOU
- Aspire to become a pharmacist or pharmacologist
- Enjoy chemistry
- Desire to help those who need maintenance drugs
- Want to work part-time, evenings, and weekends

HELPFUL PERSONAL TRAITS
- Alert and observant
- Precise and organized
- Pleasant personality
- Good communication skills
- Dedicated
- Responsible and conscientious
- Good clerical and computer skills
- Good vision and hearing

VALUE TO YOUR CAREER DEVELOPMENT
- Can help meet the values of health, helping others, love, and emotional well-being
- Satisfaction derived from patients' expression of appreciation

VALUE TO EMPLOYER/SOCIETY
- Contributes to the maintenance of good health for customers
- Pleasant and efficient service can result in growth of customer patronage and revenues for employer

POSSIBLE DOWNSIDES
- May have to climb ladders and lift heavy boxes
- Must stand for long periods

POPULATION GROUPS
- Part-Time/Temporary
- General

PREPARATION
- Formal training programs are offered at community colleges, vocational/technical schools, hospital community pharmacies, and government programs. Program length ranges from six months to two years and leads to a certificate, diploma, or associate's degree in pharmacy technology.
- Some pharmacy technicians are trained on the job
- Cannot have previous drug or substance abuse record

CERTIFICATION
- At least three states license pharmacy technicians, and all 50 states have adopted a written, standardized test for voluntary certification of technicians. Some states, including Texas and Louisiana, require certification of pharmacy technicians. Certification as a Certified Pharmacy Technician (CPhT) is offered by the Pharmacy Technician Certification Board.

RELATED JOBS/TITLES
- Pharmacy Assistant
- Pharmacy Aide
- Chemical Technician

EARNINGS
- $14,560 to $20,650 to $34,290

OUTLOOK
- According to the *Occupational Outlook Handbook,* jobs for pharmacy technicians are projected to grow much faster than the average through 2010. A strong demand is emerging for technicians with specialized training to work in specific areas, such as emergency room and nuclear pharmacy. In the future pharmacy technicians may need more education to gain certification

because of the growing number of complex medications and
new drug therapies on the market.

FOR MORE INFORMATION

*Contact AAPT for more information on membership and continuing
education. The Web site also has helpful links for those interested in
this field.*

American Association of Pharmacy Technicians (AAPT)
PO Box 1447
Greensboro, NC 27402
877-368-4771
http://www.pharmacytechnician.com

*For more information on accredited pharmacy technician training
programs, contact:*

American Society of Health-System Pharmacists
7272 Wisconsin Avenue
Bethesda, MD 20814
301-657-3000
http://www.ashp.org

To learn more about certification and training, contact:

Pharmacy Technician Certification Board
2215 Constitution Avenue, NW
Washington, DC 20037-2985
202-429-7576
http://www.ptcb.org

Pharmacy Week *is a newsletter for professionals and pharmacy students. Check the Web site for articles, industry news, job listings, and
continuing education information.*

Pharmacy Week
7 North Pinckney Street, Floor 2
Madison, WI 53703
608-251-1112
http://www.pharmacyweek.com

■ Property Manager

A property manager manages the day-to-day operations of residential or commercial property for owners. Duties may include soliciting bids and negotiating contracts related to custodial service, security, groundskeeping, trash removal, utilities, and similar services and then making recommendations to owners. Other duties include overseeing payment of rents, mortgage, taxes, insurance, and payroll; supervising maintenance of the physical structure; and writing and submitting property status reports on occupancy rates, lease expirations, and other matters. Some property managers set rental rates, resolve complaints, conduct investigations and inspections, and purchase supplies and equipment.

MAY BE GOOD FOR YOU NOW IF YOU
- Desire to be self-employed
- Have managed properties in the past
- Are looking for an investment opportunity
- Enjoy variety

HELPFUL PERSONAL TRAITS
- Computer-proficient
- Good with people
- Good negotiation skills
- Organized
- Fair
- Able to speak and write well
- Responsible
- Good at doing multiple tasks simultaneously

VALUE TO YOUR CAREER DEVELOPMENT
- Can help meet the values of achievement, variety, wealth, and independence
- Satisfaction derived from efficiently managing one or more properties
- May receive such benefits as free rental or percentage of ownership in a property

VALUE TO EMPLOYER/SOCIETY

- Can help owners maintain and improve property values and potential revenues
- Well-maintained properties tend to attract renters and buyers and positively impact the community physically and economically

POSSIBLE DOWNSIDES

- May have to put in long hours, evenings, and weekends
- May be highly stressful, particularly when complaints are difficult to resolve and tenants become irate

POPULATION GROUPS

- Job Complement
- Degree Complement
- Senior Citizen
- General

PREPARATION

- A bachelor's degree in business administration, real estate, finance, or a related area is preferred by most employers
- A background in finance, accounting, real estate, or public administration is helpful
- Professional and trade associations offer additional training in such areas as operation and maintenance of building mechanical systems, insurance and risk management, business and real estate law, and accounting and financial concepts

CERTIFICATION

- The Institute of Real Estate Management offers voluntary certification as certified property manager (CPM), accredited residential manager (ARM), real property administrator (RPA), and certified shopping center manager (CSM).

  The National Association of Residential Property Managers offers the Residential Management Professional (RMP), Master Property Manager (MPM), and Certified Residential Management Company (CRMC) designations.

  The federal government requires certification for managers of public housing that is subsidized by federal funds.

RELATED JOBS/TITLES
- Real Estate Manager
- Asset Manager
- Building Manager
- Facilities Manager
- Real Estate Agent

EARNINGS
- $16,720 to $36,020 to $80,360

OUTLOOK
- According to the *Occupational Outlook Handbook*, jobs for property managers are projected to increase faster than the average through 2010. New home developments also are increasingly organized by community or homeowner associations that require managers. In addition, more owners of commercial and multiunit residential properties are expected to use professional managers to help make their properties more profitable. The best opportunities will be for college graduates with degrees in real estate, business administration, and related fields.

FOR MORE INFORMATION
For industry information, contact:

Apartment Owners and Managers Association of America
65 Cherry Plaza
Watertown, CT 06795
860-274-2589

For information on education programs, contact:

Building Owners and Managers Association International
1201 New York Avenue, NW, Suite 300
Washington, DC 20005
202-408-2662
http://www.boma.org

For information on training programs, certification, and industry research, contact:

Institute of Real Estate Management
430 North Michigan Avenue
Chicago, IL 60611
312-329-6000
mevans@irem.org
http://www.irem.org

This organization is devoted to the multihousing industry and represents developers, owners, managers, and suppliers.

National Apartment Association
201 North Union Street, Suite 200
Alexandria, VA 22314
703-518-6141
http://www.naahq.org

For education and certification information, contact:

National Association of Residential Property Managers
PO Box 140647
Austin, TX 78714-0647
800-782-3452
http://www.narpm.org

■ Radiologic Technologist

A radiologic technologist works under the supervision of a physician and specializes in operating equipment that creates images of a patient's body tissues, organs, and bones for the purpose of medical diagnoses and therapies. Before an X-ray examination, radiologic technologists may administer drugs or chemical mixtures to the patient to better highlight internal organs. They assist patients into correct positions and protect body areas that are not to be exposed to radiation. They operate the controls to beam X rays through the patient and expose the photographic film. Radiologic technologists may also operate computer-aided imaging equipment that does not involve X rays.

MAY BE GOOD FOR YOU NOW IF YOU
- Work in a hospital setting and enjoy direct contact with patients
- Are mechanically inclined
- Have worked with photographic processes in the past

HELPFUL PERSONAL TRAITS
- Physical stamina
- Good communication skills
- Detail-oriented
- Good at following directions
- Mechanical aptitude
- Able to work well on a team

VALUE TO YOUR CAREER DEVELOPMENT
- Can help meet the values of health, helping others, and skill
- Satisfaction derived from providing a clear and accurate diagnostic tool for physicians that will significantly impact patient care

VALUE TO EMPLOYER/SOCIETY
- Contributes to the important task of acquiring accurate information on potential health problems

POSSIBLE DOWNSIDES
- Must stand for long periods
- Possible danger from overexposure to radiation

POPULATION GROUPS
- Job Complement
- General

PREPARATION
- Hospitals, medical centers, colleges and universities, and vocational and technical institutes offer training programs that range from two to four years and lead to a certificate, associate's degree, or bachelor's degree. Two-year associate's degree programs are the most popular.

CERTIFICATION
- Radiologic technologists can become certified through the American Registry of Radiologic Technologists after graduating from an accredited program in radiography, radiation therapy, or nuclear medicine.

  Radiologic technologists can receive advanced qualifications in each of the four radiography specializations: mammography, computed tomography (CT), magnetic resonance imaging (MRI), and cardiovascular interventional technology.

  Thirty-five states and Puerto Rico require radiologic technologists to be licensed.

RELATED JOBS/TITLES
- Radiographer
- X-Ray Technician
- Radiation Therapist
- X-Ray Technologist
- Diagnostic Medical Sonographer

EARNINGS
- $25,310 to $36,000 to $52,050

OUTLOOK
- According to the *Occupational Outlook Handbook,* jobs for radiologic technologists are projected to grow faster than the average through 2010. The demand for qualified technologists in some areas of the country, especially in rural areas and small towns, far exceeds the supply. Radiologic technologists who are trained to do more than one type of imaging procedure will find that they have increased job opportunities. Those specializing in sonogra-

phy are predicted to have more opportunities than those working only with radiographs. One reason for this is ultrasound's
increasing popularity due to its lack of possible side effects.

FOR MORE INFORMATION

For information on certification and programs, contact:

American Registry of Radiologic Technologists
1255 Northland Drive
St. Paul, MN 55120-1155
651-687-0048
http://www.arrt.org

*For information about the field, a catalog of educational products,
and to access their job bank, contact:*

American Society of Radiologic Technologists
15000 Central Avenue, SE
Albuquerque, NM 87123-3917
800-444-2778
http://www.asrt.org

For an educational resource guide, contact:

Society of Diagnostic Medical Sonographers
2745 N Dallas Parkway, Suite 350
Plano, TX 75093-8729
800-229-9506
sdms@sdms.org
http://www.sdms.org

■ School Counselor

A school counselor assists students in elementary, secondary, and postsecondary school and colleges and universities to make appropriate decisions. Responsibilities vary depending on the school and level, but most counselors assist with class selection and scheduling; provide information, advice, and referral services; help students to understand themselves using a variety of aids and methods; conduct individual and group counseling sessions; facilitate seminars and workshops; administer and interpret occupational-interest and personality surveys; assist with college and postsecondary preparation; keep and maintain confidential records; identify and implement intervention strategies; and provide job search and interviewing assistance. Other tasks include helping students solve problems of all types, consulting with other professionals, meeting with parents, and writing and submitting reports.

MAY BE GOOD FOR YOU NOW IF YOU
■ Desire to help students

■ Like to read and research

■ Are currently a teacher and want to enter the counseling profession

■ Are good at understanding human behavior and motivation

HELPFUL PERSONAL TRAITS
■ Strong communication skills

■ Sincere and caring

■ Empathetic

■ Organized

■ Observant and analytical

■ Detailed and accurate

■ Good listener

■ Positive and encouraging

■ Discreet

VALUE TO YOUR CAREER DEVELOPMENT
■ Can help meet the values of knowledge, wisdom, creativity, achievement, love, and helping others

■ Satisfaction derived from helping students solve a problem, succeed, or handle emotional pain

VALUE TO EMPLOYER/SOCIETY
■ May contribute to the emotional well-being of many, and helps others avoid or minimize emotional pain

■ Helps people make appropriate academic and life/career decisions

POSSIBLE DOWNSIDES
■ Can be stressful when working to resolve serious problems

■ May have large caseload and be under pressure to meet deadlines

POPULATION GROUPS
■ Degree Complement

■ Job Complement

■ Part-Time/Temporary

■ General

PREPARATION
■ The minimum requirement for a school counselor in many states is a bachelor's degree and certain stipulated courses at the graduate level

■ A master's degree in counseling or a closely related area is usually required

■ A background in teaching is necessary in many states

■ All states require state certification

■ Some states require counselors to have work experience outside of the teaching field

CERTIFICATION
■ You must be certified by your state in order to work as a school counselor. The National Board for Certified Counselors offers the National Certified Counselor (NCC) and the National Certified School Counselor (NCSC) certifications.

RELATED JOBS/TITLES

■ Counselor

■ Guidance Counselor

■ Vocational Counselor

■ Career Counselor

■ Rehabilitation Counselor

EARNINGS

■ $23,560 to $42,110 to $67,170

OUTLOOK

■ According to the *Occupational Outlook Handbook,* jobs for school counselors are projected to grow faster than the average through 2010. The federal government has called for more counselors in the schools to help address issues of violence and other dangers, such as drug use. The government, along with counseling professionals, is also working to remove the stigma of mental illness and to encourage more children and families to seek help from school counselors.

FOR MORE INFORMATION

For information about current issues in counseling and graduate school programs, contact:

American Counseling Association
5999 Stevenson Avenue
Alexandria, VA 22304
703-823-9800
http://www.counseling.org

For information about membership, publications, and professional development programs, contact:

American School Counselor Association
801 North Fairfax Street, Suite 310
Alexandria, VA 22314
800-306-4722
http://www.schoolcounselor.org

For information on certification, contact:

National Board for Certified Counselors, Inc.
3 Terrace Way, Suite D
Greensboro, NC 27403
http://www.nbcc.org

■ Underwriter

Underwriters usually work for insurance companies and determine the amount of risk or loss a firm should take with policyholders. They establish premium rates based on these calculations and write policy documents that provide coverage for risks. Tasks include analyzing applications to determine acceptability, compiling and providing supplemental reports, issuing policies, and serving as a liaison between policyholders and insurance companies.

MAY BE GOOD FOR YOU NOW IF YOU
■ Are good at calculations and making predictions based on them
■ Have worked in the past or are currently employed in the insurance business

HELPFUL PERSONAL TRAITS
■ Able to make sound judgments
■ Analytical
■ Mathematically inclined
■ Good communication skills
■ Observant
■ Computer-proficient

VALUE TO YOUR CAREER DEVELOPMENT
■ Can help to meet the values of wisdom, intellectual growth, and achievement
■ Satisfaction derived from writing a policy that is fair to all concerned parties

VALUE TO EMPLOYER/SOCIETY
■ Fair and appropriately written policies can save insurance companies significant amounts, maintain a solid client base, and attract new clients
■ Written policies protect millions of people from financial loss

POSSIBLE DOWNSIDES
■ May have to spend long periods of time at the computer, exposing you to the risks of back, arm, and wrist problems as well as eye strain

POPULATION GROUPS
- Job Complement
- Degree Complement
- General

PREPARATION
- A bachelor's degree in business administration or finance is acceptable, although any undergraduate degree is acceptable
- Accounting classes and business law classes are helpful
- To advance, continuing education is recommended

CERTIFICATION
- The Insurance Institute of America offers an Associate in Underwriting (AU) designation. The American Institute for Chartered Property Casualty Underwriters offers a more advanced professional certification, the Chartered Property and Casualty Underwriter (CPCU) designation. The American College offers the Chartered Life Underwriter (CLU) designation.

RELATED JOBS/TITLES
- Insurance Agent
- Budget Analyst
- Financial Analyst
- Claims Adjuster
- Auditor

EARNINGS
- $27,280 to $43,150 to $74,060

OUTLOOK
- According to the *Occupational Outlook Handbook,* jobs for underwriters are projected to show little or no change through 2010. The increasing use of underwriting software programs and the increasing numbers of businesses that self-insure will limit job growth in this field.

FOR MORE INFORMATION

For information regarding the CLU designation and distance education programs, contact:

The American College
270 South Bryn Mawr Avenue
Bryn Mawr, PA 19010-2196
888-263-7265
StudentServices@Amercoll.Edu
http://www.amercoll.edu

For information regarding the CPCU certification, contact:

American Institute for Chartered Property Casualty Underwriters
720 Providence Road
PO Box 3016
Malvern, PA 19355-0716
800-644-2101
http://www.aicpcu.org

For information about AU certification as well as general information about the insurance industry and underwriting, contact:

Insurance Institute of America
720 Providence Road
PO Box 3016
Malvern, PA 19355-0716
800-644-2101
http://www.aicpcu.org

For information on continuing education and general information about health underwriting, contact:

National Association of Health Underwriters
2000 North 14th Street, Suite 450
Arlington, VA 22201
703-276-0220
http://www.nahu.org

For information on life underwriting, contact:

National Association of Insurance and Financial Advisors
2901 Telestar Court
Falls Church, VA 22042-1205
703-770-8100
http://www.naifa.org

This organization is associated with The American College and has information on industry news and events.

Society of Financial Service Professionals
270 South Bryn Mawr Avenue
Bryn Mawr, PA 19010-2195
610-526-2500
http://www.financialpro.org

For information on certification and educational programs in Canada, contact:

Insurance Institute of Canada
18 King Street East, 6th Floor
Toronto, ON M5C 1C4, Canada
416-362-8586
genmail@iic-iac.org
http://www.iic-iac.org

■ Urban Planner

Urban planners develop plans for use of land as it relates to growth and restoration of communities. They work with municipal governments in addressing social, economic, and environmental issues. Duties include presenting ideas on how to use land and resources for housing, business, institutional, and recreational purposes; develop water and utility resources; develop or expand transportation services; control traffic flow; control pollution; and anticipate social impact. Other tasks may include sitting on boards and associations that address urban planning issues, writing and making oral reports, and analyzing budgets.

MAY BE GOOD FOR YOU NOW IF YOU
- Desire to work in local government
- Have worked or currently are employed in a government job
- Have the ability to visualize the big picture

HELPFUL PERSONAL TRAITS
- Good analytical and problem-solving skills
- Good communication skills
- Good judgment
- Visionary
- Good at anticipating trends
- Able to negotiate and interact with all types of people
- Good at collecting and organizing data
- Influential and persuasive

VALUE TO YOUR CAREER DEVELOPMENT
- Can help meet values of achievement, knowledge, wisdom, creativity, and helping others
- Satisfaction derived from planning an entire community

VALUE TO EMPLOYER/SOCIETY
- Helps communities to solve current problems or prevent such difficulties as urban sprawl, transportation bottlenecks, energy shortage, waste removal, crime, recreational needs, water use, and sewage concerns, among others

POSSIBLE DOWNSIDES
- Limited financial resources are often a problem for local governments
- Pressure to meet deadlines

POPULATION GROUPS
- Job Complement
- Degree Complement
- General

PREPARATION
- A bachelor's degree is the minimum requirement for most trainee jobs with federal, state, or local government boards and agencies
- A master's degree is preferred
- Certification is recommended

CERTIFICATION
- The American Institute of Certified Planners, a division of the American Planning Association, grants certification to planners who meet certain academic and professional requirements and successfully complete an examination

RELATED JOBS/TITLES
- Community Planner
- Regional Planner
- City Planner
- Geographer
- Civil Engineer

EARNINGS
- $29,800 to $46,500 to $72,080

OUTLOOK
- According to the *Occupational Outlook Handbook,* jobs for urban planners are projected to grow about as fast as the average through 2010. Urban and regional planners are needed to zone and plan land use for undeveloped and rural areas as well as for commercial development in rapidly growing suburban areas. Opportunities also exist in maintaining existing bridges, high-

ways, and sewers, and in preserving and restoring historic sites and buildings.

FOR MORE INFORMATION

For more information on careers, certification, and accredited planning programs, contact the following organizations:

American Institute of Architects
1735 New York Avenue, NW
Washington, DC 20006
800-AIA-3837
infocentral@aia.org
http://www.aia.org

American Planning Association
122 South Michigan Avenue, Suite 1600
Chicago, IL 60603
312-431-9100
APAInfo@planning.org
http://www.planning.org

For career guidance and information on student chapters as well as a list of colleges that offer civil engineering programs, contact:

American Society of Civil Engineers
1801 Alexander Bell Drive
Reston, VA 20191
800-548-2723
http://www.asce.org

To learn about city management and the issues affecting today's cities, visit this Web site or contact:

International City/County Management Association
777 North Capitol Street, NE, Suite 500
Washington, DC 20002
202-289-4262
http://www.icma.org

■ Veterinary Technician

Veterinary technicians assist veterinarians and other animal care professionals in zoos, animal hospitals, clinics, private practices, kennels, and laboratories. They care for pets and other nonfarm animals and help evaluate them for illness, disease, or injury. They are sometimes responsible for cleaning and disinfecting cages and work areas, as well as sterilizing lab and surgical tools. Other duties may include preparing animals for surgery, administering medication, and preparing lab samples.

MAY BE GOOD FOR YOU NOW IF YOU

■ Plan to become a veterinarian or pursue another animal-care profession

■ Are passionate about preventing cruelty to animals

■ Want to volunteer in an animal-related job

■ Want to work on a part-time or seasonal basis

HELPFUL PERSONAL TRAITS

■ Appreciative and respectful of animals

■ Patient

■ Good physical stamina

■ Agile

■ Manual dexterity

■ Kind and compassionate

VALUE TO YOUR CAREER DEVELOPMENT

■ Can help meet values of health, caring for animals, love, emotional well-being, and achievement

■ May develop or reinforce awareness of and compassion for animals

VALUE TO EMPLOYER/SOCIETY

■ Provides a valuable service for pet owners

■ Proper care of animals contributes to the safety, protection, and emotional well-being of many people

POSSIBLE DOWNSIDES

- Can be strenuous, noisy, unpleasant, and demanding
- May be at risk for bites, scratches, and chemical burns from accidental spills when cleaning cages
- May require lifting, crawling, and crouching
- Low wages

POPULATION GROUPS

- Part-Time/Temporary
- Ex-Offender
- General

PREPARATION

- Completion of an associate's or bachelor's degree program accredited by the American Veterinary Medical Association (AVMA)
- Any experience working with animals is an advantage

CERTIFICATION

- State codes and laws vary. Most states offer registration or certification, and the majority of these states require graduation from an AVMA-accredited program as a prerequisite for taking the examination. Most colleges and universities assist graduates with registration and certification arrangements.

   The American Association for Laboratory Animal Science offers the Assistant Laboratory Animal Technician (ALAT), the Laboratory Animal Technician (LAT), and the Laboratory Animal Technologist (LATG) designations.

RELATED JOBS/TITLES

- Animal Caretaker
- Groomer
- Animal Trainer
- Rancher
- Veterinary Assistant

EARNINGS

- $12,270 to $16,640 to $25,070

OUTLOOK

■ According to the *Occupational Outlook Handbook,* jobs for veterinary technicians are projected to grow much faster than the average through 2010. The public's love for pets coupled with higher disposable incomes will encourage continued demand for workers in this occupation.

FOR MORE INFORMATION

For information on education and certification, contact:

American Association for Laboratory Animal Science
9190 Crestwyn Hills Drive
Memphis, TN 38125
901-754-8620
http://www.aalas.org

For more information on careers, schools, and resources, contact the following organizations:

American Veterinary Medical Association
1931 North Meacham Road, Suite 100
Schaumburg, IL 60173
847-925-8070
avmainfo@avma.org
http://www.avma.org

Association of Zoo Veterinary Technicians
c/o North Carolina Zoological Park
4401 Zoo Parkway
Asheboro, NC 27203
336-879-7636
http://www.worldzoo.org/azvt

North American Veterinary Technician Association
PO Box 224
Battle Ground, IN 47920
navta@compuserve.com
http://www.avma.org/navta

For information on veterinary careers in Canada, contact:

Canadian Veterinary Medical Association
339 Booth Street
Ottawa, ON K1R 7K1 Canada
613-236-1162
http://www.cvma-acmv.org

▰ Web Developer

Web developers design and maintain Web sites for individuals, organizations, and businesses. They combine print, graphics, multimedia, and interactive features to create Web sites that are attractive, organized, easy to navigate, and up to date. Duties include programming script and graphics using various computer languages, working with other specialists to improve quality, developing technical plans, and conducting research.

MAY BE GOOD FOR YOU NOW IF YOU
▰ Have previously designed a Web page
▰ Plan to eventually become a systems analyst, programmer, or other computer-related specialist
▰ Desire to work part-time

HELPFUL PERSONAL TRAITS
▰ Creative
▰ Good at problem solving
▰ Comfortable with computers and the Internet
▰ Experienced in design, illustration, and multimedia software
▰ Artistic
▰ Able to work independently or on a team
▰ Able to work well under pressure
▰ Good at multiple tasks and time management

VALUE TO YOUR CAREER DEVELOPMENT
▰ Can help meet the values of achievement, public recognition, skill, and helping others
▰ Satisfaction derived from seeing the visual results of your work and knowing that hundreds or thousands of people are using the Web sites you created

VALUE TO EMPLOYER/SOCIETY
▰ Can help meet the shortage of workers in this area
▰ Can enhance an employer's ability to effectively compete
▰ Helps to meet the continuing demand for Web-based products and services

POSSIBLE DOWNSIDES

- May experience back, neck, or eye strain due to long periods of time at the computer
- Increased risk of arm and wrist injuries
- Isolation

POPULATION GROUPS

- Degree Complement
- Job Complement
- Senior Citizen
- General

PREPARATION

- Community colleges, colleges, and universities offer classes and certificate programs for Web developers, but there is no standard educational requirement
- A bachelor's degree in computer science, information systems, or computer programming is an advantage
- Knowledge of Internet capabilities, desktop publishing, marketing, or public relations is an asset

CERTIFICATION

- Certification is not required, but webmaster certification programs are available at many colleges, universities, and technical schools throughout the United States. Programs vary in length from three weeks to nine months or more. The International Webmasters Association and World Organization of Webmasters also offer voluntary certification programs.

RELATED JOBS/TITLES

- Webmaster
- Web Designer
- Web Site Developer
- Web Architect
- Graphic Designer
- Programmer
- Systems Analyst

EARNINGS

■ *Interactive Week's* 2001 salary survey reported that the median salary for webmasters was between $30,000 and $40,000 a year, but pay ranged from less than $20,000 to $100,000 or more. *Computerworld's* 15th Annual Salary Survey reported an average salary for webmasters of $60,244.

OUTLOOK

■ According to the U.S. Department of Labor, the field of computer and data processing services is projected to be the fastest-growing industry for the next decade. As a result, the employment rate of Web developers and other computer specialists is expected to grow much faster than the average rate for all occupations through 2010.

FOR MORE INFORMATION

For information on membership and industry-related events, contact:

Association of Internet Professionals
2629 Main Street, #136
Santa Monica, CA 90405
866-AIP-9700
info@association.org
http://www.association.org

For information on training and certification programs, contact the following organizations:

International Webmasters Association
119 East Union Street, Suite E
Pasadena, CA 91103
626-449-3709
http://www.iwanet.org

World Organization of Webmasters
9580 Oak Avenue Parkway, Suite 7-177
Folsom, CA 95630
916-608-1597
info@joinwow.org
http://www.joinwow.org

CHAPTER FOUR

WHAT'S BEST FOR YOU?

General Checklist

Would a job that requires short-term (a year or less) preparation be best for you now?

It may be if:

1. You are single, have few or no marketable skills, have never worked a full-time job, and want to establish a work record.

2. You are married, with or without children, have few or no marketable skills, and need a job almost immediately to take care of basic needs.

3. You have no education beyond high school and have a limited disability but can perform most tasks successfully.

4. You have retired from full-time employment but want to work part-time to supplement your pension and/or social security income.

5. You are a high school or college student seeking part-time employment to help offset school expenses.

6. You want to stay in good physical shape for a particular sport and want to work a physically challenging job during the summer season.

7. You have never worked for pay before and lack confidence because you are not sure how you will do.

8. You are an ex-offender and need to establish a work record and build up confidence.

9. You need to supplement the income you earn from your current full-time job.

10. You want to volunteer your time or work in a particular short-term occupation that provides exposure and experience because you hope to eventually have a related professional job that requires long-term preparation.

Would a postsecondary school certificate program be best for you now?

It may be if:

1. You have an associate's, bachelor's, or master's degree, have worked in your field for a while, and want to enrich your current skills and enhance your chances for internal advancement or promotion.

2. You already have a degree and experience but want to increase your competitive edge as you pursue another job.

3. Your boss or supervisor has strongly encouraged you to pursue certification.

4. You want to bring your skills and knowledge up to the highest level you can go in your occupational area.

5. You plan to eventually start your own business and want to be able to prove your qualifications to potential customers and clients.

6. You enjoy the challenge and satisfaction of knowing you have achieved the highest level of proficiency.

Uncertainty and frustration in regards to both present job stability and future prospects are unpleasant realities for many people today. Consequently, some workers have altered their expectations. Short-term training jobs and certification jobs may become the most popular job-hunting options in a society that has experienced significant jolts in the recent past, including the threat of terrorism and economic instability. It is a society that is likely to stay on continuous alert in preparation for other possible disruptions that make traditional long-term job preparation less practical.

Self-Assessment and Profile Sheet

A self-assessment, if honestly and thoroughly conducted, can help you uncover very helpful personal information that, too often, remains abstract and non-directive. Learning such information will more realistically help you make appropriate career decisions for this time in your life.

Note: Feel free to duplicate any of the following self-assessment sheets for your own personal use. Responses can also be simply written on a sheet of paper.

TEMPERAMENTS

Temperaments are personality attributes that relate to your way of thinking, feeling and behaving and determine whether you are comfortable or uncomfortable in a given situation. Please read the directions and complete the temperaments profile below.

Directions: Weigh each of the temperaments below on a comfort scale of 1 to 12 (1 being the situation in which you feel the MOST COMFORTABLE). Place your rating on the black line beside the appropriate letter. If you feel equally comfortable about more than one, do not hesitate to use the number twice.

___A. Situations involving a VARIETY of duties often requiring frequent CHANGE (doing different activities).

___B. Situations involving REPETITION or REPEATING SOMETHING FREQUENTLY according to set procedures or sequences (doing the same task over and over).

___C. Situations involving DOING THINGS only UNDER SPECIFIC INSTRUCTION, allowing little or no room for independent action or judgment in working out job problems (little or no personal input required).

___D. Situations that involve DEALING WITH PEOPLE in actual job duties beyond giving and receiving instructions (high degree of interaction and cooperation with people).

___E. Situations that involve DIRECTING, CONTROLLING, and PLANNING of entire activities or the activities of others.

___F. Situations involving WORKING ALONE and apart from others, although the activity may be integrated with that of others (doing most or all of your work by yourself, although it may be done around others).

___G. Situations that involve INFLUENCING PEOPLE in their opinions, attitudes, or judgments about ideas or things (being able to persuade others in the way they think, act, and behave).

___H. Situations involving PERFORMING ADEQUATELY WHILE WORKING UNDER PRESSURE or when confronted with the critical or unexpected or when taking risks (being challenged, taking challenges, and coming through on challenges).

___I. Situations that require you to make an evaluation based on PERSONAL JUDGMENT (making decisions based on personal experiences and through the use of your senses, e.g., sight, smell, hearing, taste, or touch).

___J. Situations requiring you to make a decision using MEASURABLE OR VERIFIABLE CRITERIA (making decisions based on something that has been or can be measured based on facts, rules, or standards).

___K. Situations in which you INTERPRET AND EXPRESS FEELINGS, IDEAS, OR FACTS IN A PERSONALLY CREATIVE WAY (such as through song, acting, writing, painting, etc.).

___L. Situations involving PRECISION in terms of set limits, tolerances, or standards (being detailed and exact).

PRIMARY SOURCE: *Dictionary of Occupational Titles*

STRENGTHS

Circle those you believe are most like you and rank order your strongest five.

Active	Enduring	Industrious	Punctual
Ambitious	Energetic	Intelligent	Respectful
Analytical	Enthusiastic	Joiner	Self-confident
Assertive	Expressive	Kind	Sense of humor
Affectionate	Fair	Like challenges	Sensitive
Caring	Faithful	Logical	Sharing
Charming	Flexible	Loyal	Speak well
Cheerful	Forgiving	Mannerly	Spontaneous
Comforting	Friendly	Neat	Steadfast
Compassionate	Generous	Objective	Tactful
Competent	Gentle	Observant	Talented
Cooperative	Good listener	Open-minded	Team player
Courageous	Good with hands	Optimistic	Thoughtful
Creative	Good-natured	Organized	Thrifty
Dedicated	Graceful	Patient	Tolerant
Dependable	Grateful	Peacemaker	Trustworthy
Determined	Helpful	Perform well under pressure	Understanding
Disciplined	Honest	Persistent	Unselfish
Discreet	Hospitable	Poised	Witty
Efficient	Humble	Productive	
Encouraging	Independent		

WEAKNESSES

Circle those that are most like you and rank order your weakest five.

Apathetic	Disrespectful	Liar	Racist
Argumentative	Do dumb things	Moody	Rarely finish
Aggressive	often	Not dependable	anything
Bossy	Domineering	Obnoxious	Rude
Braggart	Drug abuser	Often negative	Sarcastic
Can't concentrate	Easily offended	Overly critical	Secretive
Can't make	Fearful	Overly talkative	Selfish
decisions	Flippant	Overweight	Shy
Can't say no	Gullible	Panicky	Sickly
Can't take	Hateful	Perfectionist	Stingy
criticism	Hostile	Perform poorly	Stubborn
Clumsy	Impatient	under pressure	Stutterer
Cruel	Impulsive	Pessimistic	Sulky
Complainer	Inflexible	Picky	Tactless
Cocky	Insensitive	Poor listener	Uncouth
Condescending	Intolerant	Poor loser	Unrefined
Confronter	Irresponsible	Prejudiced	Swear a lot
Deceptive	Jealous	Prideful	Wasteful
Dependent	Judgmental	Promiscuous	Whiny
Dishonest	Lack of courage	Put things off	Wimpy
Disorganized	Lazy	Quick-tempered	Worry a lot

Top Five Strengths

1. _____
2. _____
3. _____
4. _____
5. _____

Top Five Weaknesses

1. _____
2. _____
3. _____
4. _____
5. _____

SKILLS (ABILITIES and APTITUDES)

Skills can be divided into two major categories:

ABILITIES: An ability can be defined as something you can do as a result of rehearsal and/or practice. Abilities and skills are often thought of as being the same; being skilled, though, usually implies that you can do something well. A specific knowledge of your strongest abilities can greatly increase your sense of confidence.

APTITUDES: Aptitudes are those activities you have the potential to perform well and that seem to come easily and naturally. Some people have aptitudes they are either unaware of or have been unable to develop to their fullest. Becoming aware of your aptitudes can help you to better understand who you are on the inside.

Directions: Place an "A" in front of the area(s) in which you believe you have ABILITY or APTITUDE. Feel free to write in any ability/aptitude you may have in addition to or instead of the sampling listed. Leave blank any area you are not sure of. As you go through, keep in mind that you will be asked when finished to list your five strongest abilities/aptitudes.

___Understanding instructions, facts, and underlying reasoning; being able to reason and make judgments

___Understanding the meaning of words and ideas; being able to present information or ideas clearly

___Doing arithmetic operations quickly and correctly

___Looking at flat drawings or pictures of objects and forming mental images of them in three dimensions or in terms of height, width, and depth (such as in reading blueprints, patterns, etc.)

___Observing details in pictorial or graphic material and effectively making visual comparisons; good at noticing differences in shapes, shading, etc.

___Observing details and recognizing errors in numbers, spelling, and punctuation in written materials, charts and tables; good at avoiding errors when copying

___Moving the eyes and hands or fingers together to perform a task rapidly and correctly

___Moving the fingers to work with small objects rapidly and correctly

___Moving the hands with ease and skill, as in placing and turning

___Moving hands and feet together in response to visual signals, etc.

___Seeing likenesses and differences in colors or shades; matching colors

___Finding errors in writing

___Following instruction

___Asking the right questions

___Improving what others have done

___Explaining things clearly

___Planning and organizing

___Operating mechanical equipment

___Expanding on what others have started

___Exploring and doing research

___Budgeting

___Being exact and to the point

___Spelling

___Accepting constructive advice

___Being creative

___Getting along with others

___Counseling others

___Doing artistic things

___Keeping records

___Leading and supervising others

___Teaching others

___Gardening

___Typing

___Giving others helpful advice

___Being flexible

___Drawing or designing things

___Mechanical things

___Training others to do things

___Driving vehicles

___Performing in front of others

___Taking risks

___Solving conflicts

___Noticing shapes, sizes, etc.

___Staying with a task until done

___Repairing and fixing things

___Getting others to believe in something

___Making good decisions during emergencies

___Simplifying what appears to be complex

___Learning from mistakes and past experiences

___Working alone for long periods of time

___Understanding and reading blueprints, maps, drawings, etc.

___Listening or picking up on what others say

___Seeing the underlying reasons for behavior or events

___Estimating costs

___Interpreting the feelings and emotions of others

___Reading articulately

___Doing activities that require heavy physical work

___Writing

___Copying things or activities done by others

___Collecting things

___Constructing things out of wood or metal or other materials

___Speaking in public

___Working with numbers/solving accounting-type problems

___Operating computers

___Motivating others to perform or do something

___Being thorough

___Expressing feelings

___Managing time

___Distinguishing sounds

___Doing things for others

___Communicating to others

___Controlling own emotions

___Thinking before acting

___Team sports (basketball, football, etc.)

___Individual sports (tennis, golf, etc.)

___Leading and supervising people and activities

___Using your fingers to work with small objects or instruments

___Studying English or related subjects (name related subject(s))

_____

___Studying social studies or related subjects (name related subject(s))

_____

___Studying science or related subjects (name related subject(s))

_____

___Other (include any additional or alternative skills)

_____   _____

_____   _____

_____   _____

_____   _____

List your five STRONGEST abilities/aptitudes.

1. _____

2. _____

3. _____

4. _____

5. _____

The skills list represents just a sampling of possibilities. For a more comprehensive and personalized list, you may want to read the latest edition of Richard Bolles's *What Color is your Parachute?* (Ten Speed Press, 2001).

LIFE VALUES

Life values are those deeply cherished things, activities, or relationships you place the most importance on and aspire to obtain or engage in. Life values provide us with the necessary motivation to endure many of life's hardships. Please read the directions and complete the life values survey below.

Directions: Read through the entire list. After reading, go back and place in the blank to the left of each value the code that best describes its level of importance to you (see codes below).

NVI = Not Very Important   I = Important   VI = Very Important

Next, circle the items marked VI that you consider MOST IMPORTANT (identify at least five but no more than seven).

___ACHIEVEMENT (accomplishment; being able to see or experience results which have been brought about by persistence or hard work)

___AESTHETICS (the appreciation and enjoyment of beauty for beauty's sake, as in the arts and/or in nature)

___ALTRUISM (having a special regard for or dedication to the welfare of others; service to others)

___AUTONOMY (independence; the ability to make your own decisions; self-direction; not being dependent on others)

___CREATIVITY (being able to try out new ideas; being different from the traditional; being innovative)

___EMOTIONAL WELL-BEING (having peace of mind and inner sense of security; the ability to identify and resolve inner conflict; being relatively free from anxiety)

___HEALTH (maintaining an acceptable condition in terms of your physical body; being relatively free from pain, discomfort, sickness, etc.)

___HELPING MANKIND (engaging in activities or inventing, developing, or producing something that will positively influence the lives of many; making a significant contribution of lasting or continuing value)

___HONESTY (being frank, genuine, and truthful with yourself and others)

___JUSTICE (treating others fairly or impartially; holding to truth or reason)

___KNOWLEDGE (desire to learn or know; to seek truth; to acquire information about)

___LOVE (warmth, caring, and unselfish devotion that freely accepts others without conditions)

___LOYALTY (maintaining allegiance to a person, group or institution; not abandoning; sticking with during difficult times)

___MORALITY (believing and keeping ethical standards; personal honor; integrity; doing what you truly believe is right)

___PHYSICAL APPEARANCE (concern for your attractiveness; being neat, clean, and well groomed)

___PLEASURE (having satisfaction, fun, joy, gratification)

___POWER (having possession or control; authority or influence over others)

___RECOGNITION (to be regularly recognized and positively noticed; receive attention)

___RELIGIOUS FAITH (having religious beliefs; having a personal relationship with God)

___SECURITY (being sure of most endeavors or involvements in life; having visible or concrete support or back-up before taking risks)

___SKILL (being very good at something; being better than average; performing at a high proficiency level)

___WEALTH (having many possessions and plenty of money)

___WISDOM (having mature understanding, deep insight, and good sense and judgment; being able to make appropriate and effective decisions)

WORK VALUES

Work values are those things, activities, and relationships you place the most importance on and aspire to obtain or engage in, relative to an occupation. While work values are often similar to life values, many are specifically related to an occupational setting. Work values tend to reflect much of who you are on the inside. Please read the directions and complete the work values survey below.

Directions: Read through the entire list. After reading, go back and place in the blank to the left of each value the code that best describes its level of importance to you (see codes below).

NVI = Not Very Important   I = Important   VI = Very Important

Next, circle the items marked VI that you consider MOST IMPORTANT (identify at least five but no more than seven).

___ADVANCEMENT (the ability to advance and move up; opportunity for higher position or training or education, etc.)

___ACHIEVEMENT (accomplishing something everyone can't do or will not do; doing something that requires considerable effort and/or difficulty)

___ASSISTING OTHERS (being directed and supervised by others; preferring not to have the responsibility of leading or directing people or activities)

___BENEFITS (having good hospital and life insurance, etc.; unemployment and vacation benefits)

___COMPETITION (being in an environment where you have to compete or be matched against in rivalry; being challenged to produce or perform)

___CREATIVITY (being able to try out new ideas; to be innovative)

___ENVIRONMENT (being in physical or social surroundings that are suitable to your temperaments and values, e.g., beautiful, neat, friendly, warm, etc.)

___HANDS-ON CONTACT (working with things, objects, and/or equipment; using hands and other body parts to perform tasks and activities that are primarily of a physical nature)

___HELPING OTHERS (engaging in activities that directly aid and assist others)

___INDEPENDENCE (having little or no supervision; freedom to guide your own activities and make your own decisions)

___INDUSTRY (work that keeps you busy and active continuously [could include physical and/or mental tasks]; having little or no "down time")

___INTERESTING (being positively excited and motivated most of the time in what you are doing; not likely to be bored for any significant span of time; doing something you can continuously enjoy with few exceptions)

___LEADERSHIP MANAGEMENT (being in a leadership, supervisory, or managerial position; being in charge of others)

___LEARNING (using mental abilities; gaining knowledge and understanding; being intellectually stimulated)

___MONEY (earning a high salary)

___NUMBER CONTACT (working with numbers; charting; doing statistical reports and summaries)

___POSITIVE RELATIONSHIPS (being able to get along very well with co-workers and supervisors; working with people whom you generally like; being in an environment that is characterized by warm and cooperative relationships)

___PRESTIGE (having a position that is recognized as being very important and influential by most; being in a position that commands great respect)

___PEOPLE CONTACT (high interaction and cooperation with people; being around people most of the time)

___RELIGIOUS FAITH (work that is in line with your religious beliefs; work that does not interfere with your ability to practice your religious principles)

___SECURITY (being relatively free from the fear of layoffs, job loss, reduced hours, etc.)

___SELF-DIRECTION (being able to determine what you are going to do and how you are going to do it in terms of work tasks, procedures, pace, etc.)

___SKILL (having the ability to perform one or more tasks at an extremely high proficiency level; being able to do something that requires special effort or training or education)

___SUPPORT (being in a work environment where you receive emotional support, praise, and backing)

___TRAVEL (being able to travel within a local community as well as from city to city as a part of your job responsibilities; having a travel budget)

___VARIETY (doing different things or activities; not doing repetitive tasks)

___WHOLE LIFE SENSITIVITY (working in a situation that allows or provides reasonable flexibility and choice in terms of overtime, time off, vacation selection, length of workday, family priorities, and outside concerns; being able to engage in non-job-related activities without hindrances)

___WORDS/IDEAS/INFORMATION (working with oral, visual, and written information, knowledge, facts, ideas, and/or symbols [may include numbers])

___OTHER (Include any value that has not already been mentioned. If you desire to add more, please feel free to do so.)

_____   _____

_____   _____

_____   _____

INTERESTS

Interests are those things, activities, and experiences you enjoy and are excited about. Much of what we do during our leisure time tends to reflect our interests. Interests often reveal some of our most important values. Also, you can be interested in an activity, experience, etc., without actually being involved in it. A selected list of interests and/or leisure-time activities has been included below and on the next several pages. Please read through the directions and complete the interests survey below.

Directions: Go through the entire list and circle those things, activities, or experiences that represent a STRONG INTEREST for you. Keep in mind that you will be asked when you finish to list your strongest interests.

being the leader

cooking

acting

gardening

solving math problems

visiting museums

organizing community events

working with people

water sports and games

canoeing, sailing, etc.

doing hard physical work

working with words or ideas

participating in church activities

drawing cartoons or real-life pictures

helping those who are poor

hunting, fighting, trapping, etc.

biology, life science, etc.

working on cars or other mechanical things

team sports (basketball, baseball, football, hockey, etc.)

individual sports (swimming, golf, jogging, tennis, racquetball, etc.)

reading

writing

beading

selling things

going to plays

driving vehicles

music

teaching

canning

parenting

earning money

competing with others

video games

electronic gadgets

board games

listening to the radio

watching TV

eating out

bowling

arts and crafts

traveling

antiques

talking

foreign languages

movies

politics

guns

knitting

collecting (butterflies, leaves, stamps, coins, etc.)

designing clothes

ham radio operation

interior decorating

backpacking

bird watching

camping

exploring

flying

hiking

horseback riding

nature walks

sailing

sightseeing

walking

yard work

Big Brother/Big Sister or similar program

charitable drives

counseling others

neighborhood associations

house plants and flowers

Peace Corps
military involvement
war games
Red Cross
spending time with the elderly or visiting the sick and shut in
VISTA
YMCA/YWCA
browsing through bookstores
conferences/conventions/workshops
debating
editing
jigsaw puzzles
lab experiments
lectures
organizing activities
preparing taxes
researching
science exhibits
studying and going to school
talk shows
working in nursery or day care center
writing in a diary
antique shows
art galleries
auctioning
auto shows
Bible study
boat shows
singing in a choir
playing or singing with a group
circuses
composing
concerts
macramé
needlepoint
photography
pottery
sculpting
typing

dancing
entertaining others
fairs
fashion shows
festivals
marching band
nightclubs
parties
pen-pal exchange
plays
poetry
talent shows
variety shows
visiting libraries
zoos
planetariums
4-H
archery
club leader
conservation
health
nutrition
investments
Junior Achievement
Masons
astrology
motorcycles
scouting
sororities/fraternities
broadcasting
doing housework
exercising
learning new things
comic books
magazines
newspapers
professional journals
sleeping
window shopping
shopping

teaching a craft or sport   ice skating
visiting flea markets   skiing
viewing travelogues   weightlifting
auto racing   fencing
fitness activities   cross country
gymnastics

In the blanks below, write any interests or leisure-time pursuits that you strongly enjoy but that were not included above.

_____   _____

_____   _____

_____   _____

What do you like the most? Write your STRONGEST (at least five but no more than seven) interests below.

1. _____
2. _____
3. _____
4. _____
5. _____
6. _____
7. _____

Are there any things, activities, or experiences (listed in the sampling or not) that you strongly dislike? If so, write these in the blanks below.

1. _____
2. _____
3. _____
4. _____
5. _____

SELF-ASSESSMENT PROFILE SHEET (SAPS)

A Self-Assessment Profile Sheet appears on the next page. On this sheet, record the summary information you were asked to identify in each section. If you feel there are items that should be added to the number requested because you believe they are of equal weight (or tied in terms of rank order), please feel free to do so. A sample of a completed SAPS has been included.

Remember, your profile is subject to change in time due to Significant Influencing Factors (SIF). SIF are situations or events that significantly alter your thinking patterns, activities, and relationships and consequently motivate you to make adjustments in important occupational decisions. Examples of SIF include sickness, disease, accident, flood, famine, war, change in religious beliefs, divorce, drug abuse problem, loss of a job, new legislation, among others. Therefore, it is suggested that you periodically review this profile and, whenever necessary, update it.

After completing your SAPS you will probably want to identify the occupation and/or college major you believe the results most realistically reflect (minus the weaknesses and dislikes, of course). You can generate your own list of occupations and majors to pick from or take a Career Interest Survey, such as the Kuder or Strong-Campbell surveys, from a career counselor. It is our hope that after you complete the reading and exercises in this book, as well as follow the suggestions given, you will be well on your way toward a more directed and fulfilling life.

SELF-ASSESSMENT PROFILE SHEET

LIFE VALUES

(p. 282) List the five to seven items you circled.

1.
2.
3.
4.
5.
6.
7.

WORK VALUES

(p. 283) List the five to seven items you circled.

1.
2.

3.

4.

5.

6.

7.

INTERESTS

(p. 285) List your five to seven STRONGEST interests.

1.

2.

3.

4.

5.

6.

7.

TEMPERAMENTS

(p. 276) List in order from 1 to 12 your MOST COMFORTABLE temperaments.

1.

2.

3.

4.

5.

6.

7.

8.

9.

10.

11.

12.

SKILLS

(p. 278) List your five STRONGEST abilities/aptitudes.

1.

2.

3.

4.

5.

STRENGTHS

(p. 277) List your top five strengths.

1.

2.

3.

4.

5.

WEAKNESSES

(p. 278) List your top five weaknesses.

1.

2.

3.

4.

5.

SAMPLE SELF-ASSESSMENT PROFILE SHEET

This is a sample of what a completed form might look like.

LIFE VALUES

1. Loyalty

2. Recognition

3. Honesty

4. Pleasure

5. Skill

6. Physical appearance

7. Wisdom

WORK VALUES

1. Advancement

2. Security

3. Support

4. Self-direction

5. Independence

6. Benefits

7. Words/ideas/information

INTERESTS

1. Listening to radio or watching TV
2. Working with people
3. Earning money
4. Music
5. Cooking

TEMPERAMENTS

1. Working alone
2. Precise
3. Dealing with people
4. Variety
5. Repetitive

SKILLS

1. Getting along with others
2. Asking right questions
3. Being thorough
4. Controlling my emotions
5. Keeping records

STRENGTHS

1. Dependable
2. Persistent
3. Ambitious
4. Energetic
5. Sense of humor

WEAKNESSES

1. Can't say no
2. Can't take criticism
3. Easily offended
4. Judgmental
5. Often negative

Bibliography of Print and Web Resources

PRINT RESOURCES

Farr, Michael J. *America's Top Jobs for People Without a Four-Year Degree.* 4th Edition. Indianapolis, IN: JIST, 1999.

Kerka, Sandra. "Career Certificates: High Quality and Cutting Edge?" *Career Development,* 16, no. 2 (2001): 6-7.

"Info Tech Certification." *Technical Education Resource Monitor,* 9, no. 3 (2000):1-2.

Occupational Outlook Handbook. Washington, DC: Bureau of Labor Statistics, U.S. Department of Labor, 2002-2003.

Way, Grey. *Able to Work Job Outlook,* Auburn, CA: Career Kids, 2000.

WEB RESOURCES

Career Decision Making
http://www.anselm.edu/internet/ces/decision1.html
As part of their Job Search Tutorial, the Career and Employment Service at Saint Anselm College, New Hampshire, offer self-assessment exercises at this site. While these are not standardized tests, they are available at no cost and provide a good self-assessment method.

The Career Key
http://www.ncsu.edu/careerkey
Lawrence Jones's Career Key is a vocational test designed to help you explore what career fields you may be suited for. The test can be taken online. Advice is offered on making career decisions, and links to further information are listed.

Certificate News
http://www.outreach.usf.edu/gradcerts/
This electronic newsletter compiled by Wayne Patterson has information on current developments in the area of certificate programs at the graduate, post-bachelor's, professional, undergraduate, and not-for-credit levels.

Community College Web

http://www.mcli.dist.maricopa.edu/cc/index.html

This site has links to home pages of 1,242 community colleges in the United States and a few other countries. You can search geographically, alphabetically, and by keyword.

How to Decide What to Do with Your Life

http://www.rockportinstitute.com/

This Web site contains an excerpt from Nicholas Lore's book, *The Pathfinder: How to Choose or Change Your Career for a Lifetime of Satisfaction and Success.* The author suggests how to put together your career plan one step at a time.

The Personality Page

http://www.personalitypage.com/home.html

The Myers-Briggs Type Indicator (MBTI) is a standardized test frequently used in career counseling. It identifies personal preferences in receiving and using information. There is a $10 fee for taking the assessment online one time and receiving the results. The site also provides considerable information on the personality types at no charge.

The Princeton Review Career Quiz

http://www.review.com/career/careerquizhome.cfm?careers=6

The Princeton Review offers a 24-question career quiz based on the Birkman Method, which you can learn more about at this site. The brief career quiz yields results in terms of your personality on the job and a list of occupations that may interest you. You must register to use this site, but taking the career quiz is at no charge.

RWM Vocational School Database

http://www.rwm.org/rwm/

Addresses and phone numbers of private postsecondary vocational schools in the United States can be found at this site. First select the state you're interested in and then choose the category. Among the fields represented are automotive, barbering, business, fashion design, plumbing, telecommunications, and welding. More specific occupations are included under these headings; for example, the business category includes accounting, administrative, general office, marketing, secretarial, and so on.

Occupational Index